APPETIZERS

OVER 175 MOUTHWATERING
FIRST COURSES

APPETIZERS

OVER 175 MOUTHWATERING
FIRST COURSES

Book Express

Quality and Value in Every Book…

Specially produced for Book Express, Inc.,
Airport Business Center, 29 Kripes Road,
East Granby, Connecticut, USA.

© Salamander Books Ltd., 1993

ISBN 0 86101 646 7

Recipes and photographs on the following pages are the
copyright of Merehurst Press and credited as follows:
25, 36, 37, 38, 39, 40, 41, 47 (left), 51, 52, 53, 54, 55, 56, 57, 66,
67, 68, 69, 70, 71, 72, 73, 84, 85, 86, 87, 88, 89 (left), 90, 91, 92,
93, 94, 95

All correspondence concerning the content of this volume
should be addressed to Salamander Books Ltd.,
129-137 York Way, London N7 9LG, United Kingdom.

CREDITS

Contributing authors: June Budgen, Lyn Rutherford and
Louise Steele

Introduction by: Sue Felstead

Typeset by: BMD Graphics Ltd, Hemel Hempstead

Colour separation by: Fotographics Ltd, London-Hong Kong,
J. Film Process Ltd. Bangkok, Thailand and
Scantrans Pte. Ltd, Singapore

Photographers: Per Ericson, Paul Grater and Patrick McLeavey

Printed in Italy

Contents

Introduction

Here is a fabulous collection of recipes for the start of a meal or, alternatively, for traditional Italian *Antipasti*, which is a selection of different dishes combined to make a complete meal in itself. The ideas will also appeal to anyone planning a party buffet menu for a special occasion.

To calculate the amount of food needed for a buffet for twelve, use the following menu as a guideline: one meat dish, such as Italian Meat Platter (page 45), one fish or vegetarian savory dish, such as Baked Stuffed Celery (page 19), a potato, rice or pasta salad, such as Rice-Stuffed Tomatoes (page 12), two other salad dishes from the vegetables and salads chapter, a selection of your favorite dessert recipes, including a large bowl of strawberries or raspberries, and finally, a selection of cheeses.

When presenting a platter of appetizers, make sure the plate is not crowded with too many different dishes. Often one kind of dish attractively arranged on a plate looks better than a mixture.

Buffets are suitable for a variety of different occasions and are particularly popular for barbecues, picnics, late night suppers, children's birthdays and Christenings. Appetizers for a cocktail party should be 'finger food' that can be picked up and eaten with one hand. Always ensure that napkins are provided for your guests and include a selection of both hot and cold foods. If you are planning a buffet in winter, always try to include a hot dish with cold accompaniments.

Presentation of a buffet is just as important as the food itself. To avoid a confusion of people around the table, make sure the wine and other drinks, cutlery and crockery is placed away from the food itself.

When planning party food, try to select recipes that can be cooked in advance and frozen. Simply reheat the dish just before serving. Suitable dishes for freezing include small quiches, yeast rolls and filo pastries. Any salad dish should be prepared not more than half an hour before serving to keep its freshness.

Some of the simplest appetizers to prepare are Prosciutto with Figs (page 44) or a selection of dips. Carrots, bell peppers and zucchini all make tasty scoops for tangy dips, as do cauliflowerets, mushrooms, baby sweetcorn and celery. You could also serve cheese straws or little savory crackers. There are several recipes in the final selection of this book for dips, such as Mexican Bean Dip (page 90) and Minted Sambal Dip (page 92). Alternatively, why not create your own mixture?

Most appetizers can be prepared beforehand and often taste better if they have been refrigerated before serving. If you are planning a menu, it is best to have either a simple appetizer and a more elaborate main course or vice versa. Make sure that you do not overwhelm your guests with an enormous appetizer, followed by a huge main course. Remember, first impressions are often the most lasting, and a carefully chosen appetizer can play a crucial role in any successful dinner party. Happy cooking!

INGREDIENTS

For the most part the recipes in this book call upon everyday ingredients. There are a few specialist ingredients, however, which are worth hunting for in Italian food stores to give your antipasti traditional, authentic flavors.

STORE CUPBOARD INGREDIENTS

Olive oil—the best quality is cold pressed 'Extra Virgin Olive Oil'. Arguably the best source is said to be Lucca in Tuscany but, rather like wine, olive oil will vary from individual groves and from year to year. For salads use rich, green extra-virgin olive oil (as a general rule the greener the color the richer and fruitier the flavor) but for cooking you can use a less expensive olive oil with a blander flavor which will not dominate the other flavors in a dish, or use a mixture of olive oil and either peanut or sunflower oil. A good quality olive oil can easily be flavored to give an added dimension to dressings and sauces. Try adding ingredients such as garlic, fresh herbs, lemon peel, chiles, peppercorns or other spices. A traditional example of this is 'Olio Santo' (Holy Oil) where the best extra-virgin olive oil is flavored with fresh basil and hot red chile peppers.

Olives—green olives are unripe, black ones fully ripe, you can buy them preserved in brine or in oil. They are widely available in many forms—pitted or unpitted, or stuffed with ingredients such as pimentos, anchovy fillets or almonds.

Olive paste—made from green or ripe olives ground to a paste with a little olive oil and seasonings. Olive paste can be bought in jars from supermarkets, delicatessens and Italian food stores, but it is very easy to make yourself. Simply process pitted olives in a blender or food processor, adding seasoning and just enough good quality oil to make a fairly smooth paste. Store in small jars, keep fresh and airtight by covering with a layer of olive oil. (A small jar prepared in this way can be kept, refrigerated, for about 1 month). Olive paste is delicious as a snack or simple antipasto on toast, tossed with pasta or cooked vegetables, or served as a dip.

Balsamic vinegar—more expensive than wine vinegars, but with a rich, sweet aromatic flavor. The price will vary enormously according to the length of time the vinegar has been matured. The more mature vinegars are more concentrated and so can be used very sparingly. A few drops is often all that is required to flavor a dressing.

Sun-dried tomatoes—when these are specified in a recipe those packed in oil in jars have been used. Their concentrated, salty, tomato flavor is good in salads, on bread with cheeses, and chopped into dressings and dips. Sun-dried tomatoes can also be bought loose in the dry state but they will need to be reconstituted before they are used. Put the pieces of tomato in a bowl, pour over boiling water and leave 1 to 1-1/2 hours; they will soften but still be chewy. Drain well and dry on paper towels.

Sun-dried tomato paste—with a richer flavor than ordinary tomato paste, sun-dried tomato paste is a really useful cupboard ingredient. It transforms sauces and soups and makes a quick pizza topping. Used sparingly with basil and garlic, it becomes a sauce for pasta and makes a superb savory when thinly spread on hot toasted bread.

Capers in wine vinegar—have a sharp aromatic flavor that is a perfect contrast to oily fish, eggs, fried and rich foods. Look for those preserved in wine vinegar as others can have a harsh, vinegary taste.

Red and yellow bell peppers in wine vinegar—have a sweet sour flavor. They are a useful cupboard stand-by as it is easy to use just a small piece as a garnish, cut into strips or dice. The vinegar can be used as a flavoring.

Porcini (dried ceps)—are essential for all mushroom recipes where the strong, earthy flavor of wild mushrooms is desired. Buy porcini in small packets (a little goes a long way) from Italian delicatessens and use in rice dishes, sautées and stuffings. To reconstitute before using, put the porcini in a small bowl, pour over boiling water and leave 20 to 30 minutes. Drain, reserving the soaking liquor, then rinse the porcini. Chop them for use. Use the soaking liquor, as a wonderful mushroomy stock.

1 Sun-dried tomatoes; 2 Sun-dried tomato paste; 3 Porcini mushrooms; 4 Red and yellow bell peppers in wine vinegar; 5 Capers; 6 Stuffed olives; 7 Ripe olive paste; 8 Green olive paste; 9 Green and ripe olives.

CHEESE

Mozzarella—true mozzarella is made from buffalo milk, but today most of what we buy is made from cows' milk. This is fine for cooked dishes, on pizzas and with pasta, but for salads or for eating on its own as a dessert cheese it is worth paying more for full-flavored, more creamy textured mozzarella di bufala.

Parmesan—the most famous matured hard cheese of Italy, Parmesan is most often used for grating over pasta, risottos, sauces and other cooked dishes, but it is also superb in salads and as a table cheese. Always buy Parmesan in a piece to be cut or grated as needed. The drums of ready-grated Parmesan cheese that are available simply do not compare in flavor.

Pecorino—is a hard cheese which has a fairly strong distinctive taste. It is used and eaten in the same way as Parmesan. Pecorino is available in several varieties such as Pecorino Sardo, made in Sardinia; Pecorino Romano; Pecorino Toscano; and Pecorino Pepato which is spiced with peppercorns.

Provolone—is made in a variety of shapes such as oval, cone and pear shapes which are hung by cords to ripen. Young mild 'provolone dolce' is most often eaten as a table cheese while the stronger, mature 'provolone piccante' is usually used in cooking.

Fontina—a semi-hard cheese with a natural brown rind, creamy texture and a sweet, nutty flavor. Fontina is considered a fine table cheese but it is also a good cooking cheese and its popular use is in the hot cheese fondue of the Piedmont region, 'Fonduta'.

Gorgonzola—a blue-veined cheese with a pleasantly sharp flavor made in the town of the same name in the Lombardy region of Italy.

Dolcelatte—is a factory made version of Gorgonzola. It has a milder, sweeter flavor as its name suggests—dolcelatte translates to 'sweet milk'.

Mascarpone—a fresh unripened cheese made from curdling thick cream with citric acid, heating and whipping it. It is very rich, and has a thick velvety texture. Mascarpone is available in containers in some supermarkets and delicatessens. It is often served sweetened and flavored with liqueurs as a dessert but its luxurious flavor and texture are good in savory dishes too.

SAUSAGES AND CURED MEATS

Salami—there are countless varieties of Italian salami, each region having its own specialities. Italian salamis are made of raw ingredients which are cured by brine-pickling and/or smoking. The following examples are

1 *Italian pork sausages*; 2 *Prosciutto*; 3 *Coppa di Parma*; 4 *Salami (Felino)*; 5 *Salami (Napoli)*; 6 *Bresaola*; 7 *Mortadella*.

1 *Ricotta*; 2 *Mozzarella*; 3 *Dolcelatte*; 4 *Fontina*; 5 *Parmesan*; 6 *Provolone*; 7 *Pecorino di Sardo*; 8 *Mascarpone*; 9 *Pecorino*.

available outside Italy and are well worth looking for in delicatessens and Italian food shops.

Milano—fairly fine in texture, this large salami, is made from minced pork or a mixture of pork and beef.

Varzi—coarse and highly spiced and seasoned, this salami is produced in the village of Varzi in the Parma region.

Felino—a long, thin, pork salami, coarse in texture with a good flavor. Felino is always sliced on the diagonal.

Finocchiona—a large, pure pork salami distinctively flavored with fennel seeds. It comes from Tuscany.

Prosciutto—salted and air-dried raw pork. Parma ham is the most famous of these cured meats but other regions produce their own versions.

Bresaola—sold thinly sliced, bresaola is raw beef which has been salted and air-dried in the same way as prosciutto.

Coppa di Parma—like prosciutto di Parma this is salted and air-dried raw pork but it is the shoulder cut rather than the hind leg. The flavor is slightly sweeter than prosciutto.

Mortadella—the largest and probably the most famous Italian sausage. The best mortadella is made from pure pork but others may contain some beef or organ meats. The spices and flavorings can vary and mortadella may contain whole black peppercorns, coriander seeds, pitted olives or pistachio nuts. It is usually served very thinly sliced, but it may also be diced and added to salads or cooked dishes.

BEAN & ONION SALAD

12 ounces green beans
1 onion, thinly sliced
2 tablespoons capers in wine vinegar, drained
6 tablespoons extra-virgin olive oil
Juice of 1 lemon
1/2 teaspoon hot red pepper flakes
Pinch of sugar
Salt and freshly ground pepper
2 teaspoons chopped Italian parsley
1 teaspoon chopped mint

Add beans to a saucepan of boiling salted water and cook 4 minutes until tender. Drain and refresh under cold running water. Place in a bowl with onion and capers.

Beat olive oil, lemon juice, red pepper flakes, sugar, salt and freshly ground pepper in a small bowl or shake together in a jar with a tight-fitting lid.

Pour over salad, add herbs and mix well.

Makes 4 to 6 servings.

ASPARAGUS & EGG SALAD

2 pound asparagus
Salt and freshly ground pepper
7 hard-cooked eggs
6 tablespoons olive oil
2 tablespoons white wine vinegar
2 small dill pickles, finely chopped
Freshly ground pepper
Chopped Italian parsley and Italian parsley sprig
    to garnish

Snap off and discard woody ends of asparagus stems. Using a small sharp knife, scrape stems. Rinse asparagus, then tie into small bundles using string.

Stand bundles in a deep pan of boiling salted water so tips are above water. Cover, making a dome of foil, if necessary. Boil 15 minutes until tips are crisp-tender. Drain, refresh under cold running water, drain, untie bundles and cool.

Finely chop 4 of the eggs and place in a bowl. Using a wooden spoon, gradually stir in oil, vinegar and pickles. Season with salt and freshly ground pepper. Set aside. Quarter remaining eggs and arrange with asparagus around edge of a serving plate. Pour egg sauce into center and sprinkle with chopped Italian parsley. Garnish with Italian parsley sprig.

Makes 4 to 6 servings.

BELL PEPPER SALAD

1 large red bell pepper
1 large green bell pepper
1 large yellow bell pepper
1 small red onion, sliced
16 ripe olives
2 teaspoons chopped basil or 2/3 teaspoon dried leaf
    basil
2 teaspoons chopped thyme or 2/3 teaspoon dried leaf
    thyme
DRESSING:
3 tablespoons extra-virgin olive oil
1 tablespoon red wine vinegar
1 garlic clove, finely chopped
Pinch of sugar
Salt and freshly ground pepper

To make dressing, mix all ingredients together in a small bowl, or shake together in a jar with a tight-fitting lid. Set aside. Preheat broiler. Place whole peppers under hot broiler about 10 minutes, turning occasionally, until skins are evenly blistered and blackened. Transfer peppers to a plastic bag a few minutes, then peel away and discard skins.

Cut peppers in half, remove and discard seeds and cut peppers into strips. Place in a salad bowl with onion and olives. Stir or shake dressing and pour over salad. Toss gently to mix and sprinkle with herbs.

Makes 4 servings.

MUSHROOMS & LIMA BEANS

1-1/3 cups dried lima beans, soaked overnight, and
    drained
3 cups thinly sliced button mushrooms
2-ounce piece Parmesan cheese
1 tablespoon finely chopped Italian parsley
Lettuce leaves and Italian parsley sprigs to garnish
DRESSING:
5 tablespoons extra-virgin olive oil
Finely grated peel of 1/2 lemon
1/2 teaspoon whole-grain mustard
Pinch of sugar
Salt and freshly ground pepper

Put beans in a large saucepan with enough water to cover. Bring to a boil and boil briskly 10 minutes, then reduce heat and simmer 40 to 45 minutes or until beans are tender. Drain and rinse under cold running water. Drain well and leave until cold. To make dressing, mix all ingredients together in a small bowl or shake together a jar with a tight-fitting lid. Set aside.

Put beans and mushrooms in a large serving bowl. Add dressing and toss well to mix. Let stand up to 2 hours, if desired. Using a small, sharp knife, pare wafer-thin slices of cheese, add to salad and toss lightly to mix. Sprinkle with chopped Italian parsley, garnish with lettuce leaves and Italian parsley sprigs and serve immediately.

Makes 6 servings.

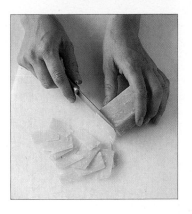

MIXED BEAN SALAD

2/3 cup dried cannelini beans, soaked overnight and drained
2/3 cup dried black-eyed peas, soaked overnight and drained
2/3 cup dried lima beans, soaked overnight and drained
1 small onion, chopped
2 tablespoons chopped oregano or 2 teaspoons dried leaf oregano
1 tablespoon chopped Italian parsley
Italian parsley sprig to garnish
DRESSING:
1/4 cup extra-virgin olive oil
2 tablespoons red wine vinegar
2 garlic cloves, crushed
Salt and freshly ground pepper

Place beans in separate pans. Cover with cold water, bring to a boil and boil briskly 10 minutes, then reduce heat and simmer, covered, about 1 hour until just tender. Drain, rinse briefly under cold running water, then drain and transfer to a serving dish.

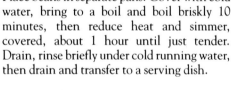

To make dressing, mix all ingredients together in a small bowl or shake together in a jar with a tight-fitting lid. Add onion and dressing to beans while they are warm. Stir and cool to room temperature. Cover and chill until served. Just before serving, stir in oregano and parsley and adjust seasoning. Garnish with Italian parsley sprig.

Makes 6 servings.

RICE-STUFFED TOMATOES

6 large, ripe tomatoes
2/3 cup risotto rice or long-grain white rice
1-1/2 cups boiling chicken stock
4 tablespoons olive oil
1 small onion, finely chopped
1 garlic clove, crushed
1/2 pound fresh spinach, finely chopped
3 tablespoons chopped Italian parsley or fennel
Salt and freshly ground pepper
Mixed lettuce leaves to serve

Cut tops off tomatoes and reserve. Using a teaspoon scoop out seeds and flesh from tomatoes; reserve seeds and flesh for use in sauces or casseroles.

Place tomatoes upside down to drain. Preheat oven to 350F (175C). Rinse rice and put in a small saucepan with boiling chicken stock. Bring to a boil, then reduce heat, cover and simmer 12 to 15 minutes until liquid is absorbed. If rice is not tender, stir in a little boiling water and continue cooking. Meanwhile, heat 2 tablespoons of the oil in a medium-size saucepan. Add onion and garlic and saute 3 minutes to soften.

Stir in spinach, parsley or fennel and cooked rice. Remove from heat and season with salt and freshly ground pepper. Sprinkle insides of tomatoes with a little salt and fill with rice mixture. Replace reserved tomato tops. Arrange in a baking dish and sprinkle with remaining oil. Bake in the preheated oven 20 minutes until tomatoes are tender. Serve hot or cold with lettuce leaves.

Makes 6 servings.

EGGPLANT NAPOLETANA

1-1/2 pounds medium-size Japanese-type eggplant
Salt
1 cup all-purpose flour
1 cup peanut oil
1 cup olive oil
1/2 cup extra-virgin olive oil
6 anchovy fillets in oil, drained and mashed
1 tablespoon sun-dried tomato paste
3 tablespoons red wine vinegar
8 Italian parsley sprigs
2 garlic cloves
Freshly ground pepper
Italian parsley sprigs to garnish

Preheat peanut oil and olive oil together in a saucepan or deep-fryer to 375F (190C). Deep-fry eggplant in batches in the hot oil about 4 minutes until golden-brown. Transfer to paper towels to drain. Keep hot.

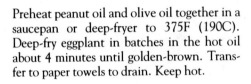

Peel the eggplants and cut into 1-inch slices. Spread eggplant out on a large plate and sprinkle with salt. Leave 30 minutes, then rinse thoroughly under cold running water to remove salt, drain and pat dry with paper towels.

In a small saucepan, gently warm the extra-virgin oil over low heat. Stir in anchovies, tomato paste and vinegar and simmer, stirring, 2 minutes.

Put flour into a large plastic bag, add eggplant and toss to coat. Remove coated eggplant and discard excess flour.

Finely chop together the parsley sprigs and garlic. Transfer eggplant to a warmed serving plate. Top with anchovy sauce and season with salt and freshly ground pepper. Sprinkle with chopped parsley and garlic and serve immediately garnished with Italian parsley sprigs.

Makes 4 to 6 servings.

—BROCCOLI & PROSCIUTTO —

1-1/2 pounds broccoli
1/2 pound tomatoes
3 tablespoons olive oil
5 ounces prosciutto, cut into strips
2 garlic cloves, chopped
1/3 cup pine nuts, toasted
12 pitted ripe olives, halved
Salt and freshly ground pepper
Handful of basil leaves

Divide the broccoli into flowerets. Add to a saucepan of boiling salted water and cook about 4 minutes, until crisp-tender. Drain, refresh under cold running water, then drain well.

Meanwhile, put tomatoes in a bowl and add boiling water to cover. Leave about 30 seconds, then drain, cool with cold water and peel away skins. Cut the tomatoes into chunks and discard the seeds. Heat 2 tablespoons of the oil in a skillet. Add prosciutto and garlic and cook over high heat 2 to 3 minutes until prosciutto is crisp. Using a slotted spoon transfer prosciutto to a plate and keep warm.

Add remaining oil to pan with tomatoes, pine nuts and olives. Cook, stirring, 1 minute. Stir in broccoli and prosciutto and heat through briefly, gently stirring. Season with salt and freshly ground pepper. Transfer to a warmed serving dish and sprinkle with basil leaves. Serve hot.

Makes 4 to 6 servings.

—BAKED STUFFED ARTICHOKES —

4 large artichokes
1 tablespoon butter
5 tablespoons olive oil
3 slices lean bacon, chopped
1 small onion, finely chopped
2 celery stalks, finely chopped
2 medium-size zucchini, finely chopped
1 garlic clove, crushed
1 tablespoon chopped sage or 1 teaspoon dried sage
1 tablespoon chopped Italian parsley
Salt and freshly ground pepper
3 tablespoons fresh bread crumbs
1/4 cup shredded pecorino cheese (1 ounce)
Juice of 1 lemon
Italian parsley sprigs to garnish

Preheat oven to 400F (205C). Cook artichokes in a saucepan of boiling salted water 30 minutes. Remove and place upside down to drain. Pull away and discard outer leaves and, using a teaspoon, remove central hairy choke. Heat butter and 2 tablespoons of the olive oil in a saucepan. Add bacon, onion, celery, zucchini and garlic and cook 5 minutes, stirring frequently, until vegetables are just soft. Stir in herbs. Puree half the mixture in a blender or food processor fitted with the metal blade. Return to pan. Season with salt and freshly ground pepper.

Place artichokes close together in baking dish. Fill center of artichokes with vegetable mixture. In a small bowl, mix together bread crumbs and cheese. Pile on top of filling. Sprinkle with lemon juice and remaining 3 tablespoons olive oil. Cover with foil and bake in preheated oven 15 minutes. Remove foil. Bake 10 minutes until lightly browned. Garnish with Italian parsley sprigs.

Makes 4 servings.

STUFFED ARTICHOKE BOTTOMS

—CAULIFLOWER INSALATA—

6 hard-cooked eggs, finely chopped
7 to 9 tablespoons extra-virgin olive oil
2 tablespoons white wine vinegar
1/2 red bell pepper packed in wine vinegar, drained and chopped
2 tablespoons capers in wine vinegar, drained and chopped
2 tablespoons chopped Italian parsley
Salt and freshly ground pepper
1 (14-oz) can artichoke bottoms, drained
3 tablespoons extra-virgin olive oil
Juice of 1/2 lemon
1 teaspoon coriander seeds, crushed
Italian parsley sprigs to garnish

1 cauliflower
1/3 cup pitted green olives, halved
1/3 cup pitted ripe olives, halved
2 tablespoons capers in wine vinegar, drained
1 red bell pepper packed in wine vinegar, drained and chopped
5 anchovy fillets canned in oil, drained and halved crosswise
6 tablespoons extra-virgin olive oil
1 tablespoon white wine vinegar
Salt and freshly ground pepper
3 small carrots

Break the cauliflower into flowerets.

Place eggs in a bowl then, using a wooden spoon, gradually stir in 4 tablespoons of the oil and the vinegar; the mixture should be stiff enough to hold its shape but if too dry add a little more olive oil. Stir in bell pepper, capers and parsley and season with salt and freshly ground pepper.

Add cauliflower to a saucepan of boiling salted water and boil 4 to 5 minutes until crisp-tender. Drain, refresh under cold running water, drain again and cool. Put into a serving bowl with olives, capers, bell pepper and anchovies. Add oil and vinegar and season with salt and freshly ground pepper. Toss gently to mix and refrigerate at least 30 minutes.

Divide egg mixture among artichoke bottoms and arrange on a serving plate. Drizzle with the 3 tablespoons olive oil and lemon juice and sprinkle with coriander seeds. Cover and refrigerate at least 1 hour. Serve garnished with Italian parsley sprigs.

Makes 4 to 6 servings.

Using a vegetable peeler, remove long thin slices from carrots. Place slices in a bowl of iced water 10 minutes to curl and crisp. Drain thoroughly and add to salad. Toss lightly to mix, then serve.

Makes 6 servings.

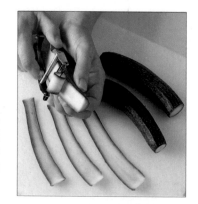

FUNGHETTO

1 eggplant (about 8 ounces), diced
2 cups thinly sliced zucchini (about 8 ounces)
Salt
1/2 ounce dried porcini mushrooms
2 tablespoons butter
1/4 cup olive oil
2 garlic cloves, crushed
4 cups sliced button or oyster mushrooms or a mixture (8 ounces)
2 tablespoons rosemary leaves
2 tablespoons chopped Italian parsley
Freshly ground pepper
Rosemary sprig to garnish

Put eggplant and zucchini into a colander. Sprinkle with salt and drain 30 minutes.

Rinse thoroughly to remove salt and drain on paper towels. Put dried mushrooms into a small bowl. Cover with warm water and soak 20 minutes. Strain, reserving 3 tablespoons soaking liquid. Rinse thoroughly and chop.

Heat butter and oil in a large heavy skillet. Add garlic and saute 1 minute. Add eggplant, zucchini, fresh and dried mushrooms and rosemary. Saute 3 to 4 minutes. Stir in reserved porcini soaking liquor and the parsley, reduce heat and cook 20 minutes until vegetables are soft and liquid evaporated. Season with salt and freshly ground pepper. Garnish with rosemary sprig.

Makes 4 to 6 servings.

ZUCCHINI WITH GARLIC

6 medium-size zucchini
1 cup corn oil or peanut oil
1 cup light olive oil
2 garlic cloves, finely chopped
1/3 cup red wine vinegar
1 to 2 tablespoons chopped dill
Salt and freshly ground pepper
12 mint leaves

Preheat oven to 375F (190C). Using a vegetable peeler and pressing quite firmly, peel along the length of the zucchini to remove long thick strips. Divide between 2 baking sheets; bake 20 minutes until crisp-tender.

Transfer zucchini to paper towels to drain 30 minutes. Preheat the oils together in a saucepan or deep-fryer to 375F (190C). Line a baking sheet with paper towels. Fry zucchini slices in batches in the hot oil 2 to 3 minutes until light golden-brown. Transfer to paper towels to drain. When all the zucchini are cooked and drained transfer to a serving dish.

Add garlic, wine vinegar, dill, salt and freshly ground pepper to zucchini. Toss gently to mix. Cover and refrigerate at least 2 hours. Serve sprinkled with mint leaves.

Makes 6 servings.

MUSHROOMS WITH MARSALA

1/4 cup butter
6 cups thickly sliced large button mushrooms
(about 1 pound)
2 garlic cloves, sliced
2/3 cup marsala wine
Salt and freshly ground pepper
Chopped Italian parsley and Italian parsley leaves
to garnish

Preheat oven to 375F (190C). Use butter to grease a large flat baking dish.

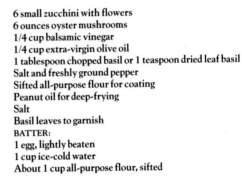

Layer mushrooms in dish and sprinkle with garlic.

Pour marsala over mushrooms and season with salt and freshly ground pepper. Bake in preheated oven 25 to 30 minutes until mushrooms are tender. Serve hot or cold sprinkled with chopped Italian parsley and Italian parsley leaves.

Makes 4 servings.

Note: For a special occasion or a treat, substitute fresh porcini mushrooms for some of the button mushrooms.

ZUCCHINI-MUSHROOM FRITTERS

6 small zucchini with flowers
6 ounces oyster mushrooms
1/4 cup balsamic vinegar
1/4 cup extra-virgin olive oil
1 tablespoon chopped basil or 1 teaspoon dried leaf basil
Salt and freshly ground pepper
Sifted all-purpose flour for coating
Peanut oil for deep-frying
Salt
Basil leaves to garnish
BATTER:
1 egg, lightly beaten
1 cup ice-cold water
About 1 cup all-purpose flour, sifted

Break flowers off zucchini.

Slice each zucchini lengthwise into three strips. Cut large mushrooms into halves or quarters; leave others whole. Place vinegar in a small bowl for dipping. In a separate small bowl mix together olive oil, basil, salt and freshly ground pepper. Set both aside. To make batter, in a small bowl, stir together egg and water. Gently mix in enough flour to give batter the consistency of light cream.

Half fill a deep-fryer or saucepan with oil and preheat to 350F (175C). Dip zucchini strips and flowers and mushrooms into sifted flour to coat. Shake off excess. Dip a few pieces of floured vegetables at a time in batter, then deep-fry in hot oil 3 to 4 minutes, turning frequently, until golden. Drain on paper towels. Season with salt. Garnish with basil leaves. Serve with the bowls of balsamic vinegar and flavored oil.

Makes 4 to 6 servings.

PEPERONATA

ARUGULA & PINE NUT SALAD

2 green bell peppers
1 red bell pepper
1/3 cup olive oil
1 onion, coarsely chopped
1 garlic clove, crushed
1-1/2 pounds tomatoes, peeled, seeded and chopped
Pinch of sugar
Salt and freshly ground pepper
1 tablespoon chopped Italian parsley
Italian parsley sprig to garnish

Preheat broiler. Place whole peppers under hot broiler about 10 minutes, turning occasionally, until skins are evenly blistered and blackened.

Transfer to a plastic bag a few minutes, then peel away and discard skins. Cut peppers in half, remove and discard seeds and cut peppers into strips. Heat oil in a large skillet over medium heat. Add onion and garlic and cook 3 minutes to soften. Stir in tomatoes and sugar and cook 10 to 12 minutes until thickened.

Add pepper strips and simmer 5 minutes until peppers are soft. Season with salt and freshly ground pepper and serve hot sprinkled with chopped Italian parsley and garnished with Italian parsley sprig.

Makes 4 servings.

1/3 cup pine nuts
4 ounces arugula
4 green onions, thinly sliced
8 chervil sprigs, coarsely torn
2 thin slices prosciutto, cut into strips
DRESSING:
Juice of 1 lemon
3 tablespoons extra-virgin olive oil
1 tablespoon walnut oil
1/2 teaspoon Dijon-style mustard
Salt and freshly ground pepper

In a small saucepan, heat the pine nuts over medium-high heat, stirring constantly, about 3 minutes until golden-brown.

Remove to a plate and set aside to cool. Place arugula, green onions and chervil in a serving bowl. Toss gently to mix.

To make dressing, mix ingredients together in a small bowl or shake together in a jar with a tight-fitting lid. Pour over salad and toss. Sprinkle with reserved pine nuts.

Makes 4 to 6 servings.

TOMATO & RED ONION SALAD

BAKED STUFFED CELERY

4 beefsteak tomatoes, sliced
4 sun-dried tomatoes packed in oil, drained and
    chopped
1 red onion, chopped
Salt and freshly ground pepper
3 tablespoons extra-virgin olive oil
2 tablespoons oil from the sun-dried tomatoes
2 tablespoons red wine vinegar
Pinch of sugar
4 tablespoons chopped mixed fresh herbs such as basil,
    oregano, parsley, chives, dill and cilantro
Herb sprigs to garnish

1 head celery separated into stalks and cut into 3-inch
    lengths
1/4 cup olive oil
STUFFING:
3 tablespoons olive oil
1 small onion, finely chopped
1 garlic clove, chopped
2 tablespoons capers in wine vinegar, drained
1 red bell pepper packed in wine vinegar, drained and
    chopped
1/2 cup fresh bread crumbs
1/2 cup grated provolone cheese (2 ounces)
3 tablespoons chopped Italian parsley
Salt and freshly ground pepper
Italian parsley to garnish

Layer tomatoes, sun-dried tomatoes and onion in a shallow serving dish. Season with salt and freshly ground pepper.

Preheat oven to 375F (190C). Add celery to a large saucepan of boiling water and cook 3 minutes. Drain and refresh under cold running water. Drain on paper towels. To make stuffing, heat oil in a skillet. Add onion and garlic and cook 3 minutes to soften. Remove from heat. Chop together capers and bell pepper, then stir into skillet with bread crumbs, cheese and the 3 tablespoons parsley. Season with salt and freshly ground pepper.

Mix together remaining ingredients except herb sprigs in a small bowl, then pour over salad. Garnish with herb sprigs.

Makes 4 to 6 servings.

Place stuffing in cavities of celery pieces. Arrange celery with stuffing up, in one layer in a shallow baking dish. Drizzle with oil. Cover with foil and bake in preheated oven 20 minutes. Remove foil and continue cooking about 10 minutes until celery is tender and stuffing lightly browned. Serve hot or warm, garnished with Italian parsley.

Makes 6 servings.

TRICOLOR SALAD

1 avocado
2 tablespoons lemon juice
2 large beefsteak tomatoes, sliced
6 ounces Italian mozzarella cheese, preferably made
   from buffalo milk
Salt and freshly ground pepper
Few drops balsamic vinegar
1/4 cup extra-virgin olive oil
6 fresh basil leaves, shredded
Basil sprigs to garnish

Seed and peel avocado, slice thinly and brush with lemon juice.

Arrange tomatoes, cheese and avocado on a large plate. Season with salt and freshly ground pepper.

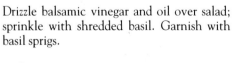

Drizzle balsamic vinegar and oil over salad; sprinkle with shredded basil. Garnish with basil sprigs.

Makes 4 to 6 servings.

ZUCCHINI & TOMATO SALAD

About 30 (2-inch-long) zucchini (about 1 pound total)
12 ounces small tomatoes, sliced
4 green onions, white part only, finely chopped
1 tablespoon chopped Italian parsley
Italian parsley sprig to garnish
DRESSING:
5 tablespoons extra-virgin olive oil
3 tablespoons white wine vinegar
2 garlic cloves, chopped
1 tablespoon chopped thyme or 1 teaspoon dried leaf
   thyme
1 teaspoon honey
Salt and freshly ground pepper

Add zucchini to a saucepan of boiling salted water and cook 3 minutes. Drain well. Using a small, sharp knife, cut a long lengthwise slit in each zucchini, place in a serving dish.

To make dressing, mix ingredients together in a small bowl or shake together in a jar with a tight-fitting lid. Pour over hot zucchini and leave until completely cold. Add tomatoes, green onions and parsley to dish. Toss to mix. Adjust seasoning before serving. Garnish with Italian parsley sprig.

Makes 6 servings.

FENNEL & DOLCELATTE

3 medium-size fennel bulbs
1 tablespoon fennel seeds, lightly crushed
1/4 cup extra-virgin olive oil
Juice of 1/2 lemon
Pinch of sugar
Salt and freshly ground pepper
1 cup crumbled dolcelatte cheese

Trim fennel, reserving green feathery tops. Add whole bulbs to saucepan of boiling salted water. Cook 5 minutes, then drain. Refresh under cold running water, drain well and pat dry with paper towels. Set aside. Chop reserved fennel tops and set aside.

In a small skillet over medium heat, dry-fry seeds 2 to 3 minutes to brown and release aroma. Remove from heat and stir in olive oil, lemon juice, sugar, salt and freshly ground pepper.

Thinly slice fennel bulbs and arrange in a shallow serving dish. Add oil and fennel seed mixture. Sprinkle with cheese and reserved fennel tops. Let stand 30 minutes. Toss lightly before serving.

Makes 4 to 6 servings.

EGG & ARTICHOKE SALAD

4 hard-cooked eggs, quartered
12 artichoke hearts in oil, drained
12 stuffed green olives, halved
2 tablespoons capers in wine vinegar, drained
1 tablespoon chopped Italian parsley
1 tablespoon chopped oregano or 1 teaspoon dried leaf oregano
Italian parsley leaves to garnish
DRESSING:
5 tablespoons extra-virgin olive oil
2 tablespoons white wine vinegar
1 teaspoon Dijon-style mustard
1 teaspoon finely grated lemon peel
1 teaspoon honey
Salt and freshly ground pepper

Arrange eggs on a serving plate with artichokes and olives. Sprinkle with capers and herbs.

To make dressing, mix all ingredients together in a small bowl, or shake together in a jar with a tight-fitting lid. Pour over salad and serve at once garnished with Italian parsley leaves.

Makes 4 to 6 servings.

Note: Artichoke hearts in oil are similar, but far superior, to canned artichoke hearts. They are available at Italian delicatessens.

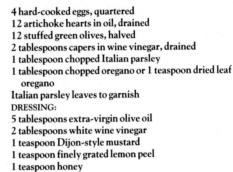

EGGPLANT WITH TOMATO SAUCE

8 to 10 small Japanese-type eggplant (about 1 pound total)
Salt
6 tablespoons extra-virgin olive oil
1 shallot, finely chopped
2 garlic cloves, crushed
1 pound tomatoes, peeled and finely chopped
2 oregano sprigs
1/3 cup red wine
1 tablespoon sun-dried tomato paste
1 tablespoon chopped Italian parsley
Freshly ground pepper
Italian parsley sprigs or basil sprigs to garnish

Meanwhile, heat 2 tablespoons of the oil in a small saucepan, add shallot and garlic and cook 3 to 4 minutes to soften. Stir in tomatoes and oregano and cook 1 minute.

Leaving stem end intact, slice eggplant lengthwise from blossom end almost to stem end 3 or 4 times so they can be flattened out to give a fanned appearance.

Add wine and tomato paste and bring to a boil. Reduce heat and simmer sauce, covered, 10 minutes, stirring frequently until vegetables are tender. Discard oregano, stir in parsley and season with salt and freshly ground pepper.

Place in a shallow dish, sprinkle with salt and leave 25 to 30 minutes. Rinse thoroughly to remove salt. Drain and pat dry with paper towels; set aside. Preheat broiler.

Arrange eggplant on a baking sheet. Press each eggplant to fan out slices. Brush with remaining 4 tablespoons olive oil and cook under hot broiler 5 to 6 minutes, turning once, until tender and beginning to brown. Serve immediately with hot sauce. Garnish with Italian parsley or basil sprigs.

Makes 4 to 6 servings.

— EGGPLANT & OLIVE SALAD —

2 Japanese-type eggplants, diced
Peanut oil for deep-frying
6 tablespoons light olive oil
2 onions, chopped
1 garlic clove, chopped
4 celery stalks, sliced
2 small zucchini, sliced
1 tablespoon chopped rosemary
1 (14-oz.) can chopped plum tomatoes
1 tablespoon sun-dried tomato paste
2 teaspoons sugar
1/3 cup red wine vinegar
1 cup pitted mixed olives, halved
2 tablespoons capers in wine vinegar, drained
Salt and freshly ground pepper
Italian parsley sprig to garnish

Put eggplant in a colander, sprinkle with salt and drain 30 to 40 minutes. Rinse thoroughly to remove salt, drain and pat dry with paper towels. Heat peanut oil in a large skillet over high heat. Add eggplant and fry 4 to 5 minutes until an even golden-brown. Transfer eggplant to paper towels. Transfer to a serving dish and set aside. Heat olive oil in a large skillet over medium heat, add onions and garlic and cook 5 minutes to soften.

Add celery, zucchini and rosemary and cook 5 minutes. Stir in plum tomatoes, tomato paste, sugar and vinegar and cook, stirring frequently, 10 minutes until vinegar has evaporated. Transfer to serving dish and cool. Add olives and capers to serving dish. Season with salt and freshly ground pepper and toss well to mix. Cover and refrigerate before serving. Garnish with Italian parsley sprig.

Makes 4 to 6 servings.

— CANNELINI BEAN PASTE —

1-1/4 cups dried cannelini beans, soaked overnight, drained
4 cups water
1/2 teaspoon hot red pepper flakes
2 teaspoons tomato paste
2 rosemary sprigs
2 tablespoons butter
2 tablespoons extra-virgin olive oil
1 garlic clove, finely chopped
1 tablespoon finely chopped oregano or 1 teaspoon dried leaf oregano
3/4 to 1 cup hot chicken stock
Juice of 1 small lemon
Salt and freshly ground pepper
Rosemary sprigs to garnish
Toasted bread or vegetable sticks to serve

Combine beans in a saucepan with the water, red pepper flakes, tomato paste and rosemary sprigs. Bring to a boil, then reduce heat, cover and simmer 2 hours until most of the water has been absorbed and beans are very tender. Discard rosemary. In a blender or food processor fitted with the metal blade, puree beans and remaining liquid until very smooth.

Heat butter and oil in a medium-size saucepan. Add garlic and oregano. Cook 2 minutes. Stir in bean puree and hot stock and simmer 10 to 12 minutes, stirring frequently, until mixture is very thick. Remove from heat, stir in lemon juice and season with salt and freshly ground pepper. Garnish with rosemary sprigs. Serve either hot spread on toasted crusty bread or cold with fresh vegetable sticks or warmed crusty bread.

Makes 6 servings.

MARINATED MUSHROOMS

1 pound mushrooms such as button, porcini, oyster or
   shiitake
1-1/4 cups white wine vinegar
1-1/4 cups water
2 small fresh red chiles, halved lengthwise and seeded
Grated peel of 1 lemon
2 bay leaves
2 teaspoons coriander seeds
1 teaspoon cumin seeds
1 teaspoon peppercorns
3 garlic cloves, sliced
About 1-1/4 cups olive oil

Thickly slice large mushrooms, leave others
whole. Put vinegar, water, chiles, lemon
peel, bay leaves, coriander seeds, cumin seeds
and peppercorns into a medium-size saucepan. Bring to a boil, then add the mushrooms
and boil 7 to 8 minutes until tender. Drain
and discard liquid. Spread mushrooms and
spices on paper towels to dry.

Fill a 2-1/2 cup canning jar with boiling
water, pour out water and place jar in a warm
oven to dry. Fill jar with mushroom mixture
and garlic slices. Add oil, making sure mushrooms are completely covered. Seal tightly
and marinate 5 days in the refrigerator.

Makes about 2-1/2 cups.

MARINATED OLIVES

2-3/4 cups ripe olives (1 pound)
1 fresh red chile, seeded, chopped
3 garlic cloves, chopped
2 thyme sprigs
2 tablespoons dill seeds, lightly crushed
Salt and freshly ground pepper
Olive oil to cover
2 tablespoons chopped dill

Using a small sharp knife make a lengthwise
slit through to the pit of each olive.

Put olives in a bowl with chile, garlic, thyme
and dill seeds. Season with salt and freshly
ground pepper. Add enough olive oil to just
cover. Cover bowl and refrigerate 3 to 14
days.

Drain olives; reserve oil for cooking or salad
dressings. Discard thyme sprigs. Serve olives
sprinkled with chopped dill.

Makes 6 servings.

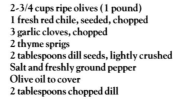

SHRIMP VOL-AU-VENTS

ANCHOVY BEIGNETS

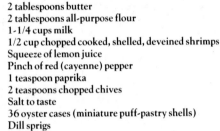

2 tablespoons butter
2 tablespoons all-purpose flour
1-1/4 cups milk
1/2 cup chopped cooked, shelled, deveined shrimps
Squeeze of lemon juice
Pinch of red (cayenne) pepper
1 teaspoon paprika
2 teaspoons chopped chives
Salt to taste
36 oyster cases (miniature puff-pastry shells)
Dill sprigs

Melt butter in a saucepan over low heat. Stir in flour; cook, stirring constantly, 2 minutes. Remove from heat, add milk all at once, stirring constantly.

Return to the heat and continue to cook, stirring, until sauce boils and thickens. Remove from heat. Stir in shrimps, lemon juice, red pepper, paprika and chives. Season with salt. Cool slightly. Preheat oven to 400F (200C).

1/4 cup butter, cut in pieces
1/2 cup water
1/2 cup all-purpose flour
4 canned flat anchovy fillets, drained, mashed
2 eggs
2 tablespoons slivered almonds
Vegetable oil for deep-frying

In a medium saucepan, heat water and butter until melted, stirring; bring to a fast boil.

Add flour all at once. Stir over a low heat for about 1 minute or until mixture leaves sides and forms a ball; remove from heat and cool slightly. Beat in anchovy fillets, then beat in eggs, 1 at a time, beating until smooth after each addition. Stir in slivered almonds.

Fill oyster cases evenly with shrimp mixture. Arrange on baking sheets and bake 10 minutes. If vol-au-vents are extremely hot, cool slightly before serving. Garnish with dill sprigs. Provide small napkins.

Makes 36.

In a deep, heavy saucepan, heat about 2 inches of oil to 375F (190C) or until a 1-inch bread cube turns golden brown in about 50 seconds. Add a few teaspoons of the anchovy mixture at a time, and cook until golden on all sides. Drain on paper towels. Serve warm. Provide small napkins.

Makes 12 to 15.

DEEP-FRIED SMALL FISH

MUSSEL & FENNEL SALAD

8 ounces small fish such as anchovies and young
    sardines
1/2 cup all-purpose flour
2 teaspoons finely chopped Italian parsley
Salt and freshly ground pepper
Peanut oil for deep-frying
Lemon slices to serve

Rinse fish thoroughly, drain and pat dry on
paper towels.

Put flour, parsley, salt and freshly ground
pepper into a plastic or paper bag and shake to
mix. Add fish in batches and shake gently to
coat.

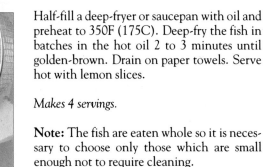

Half-fill a deep-fryer or saucepan with oil and
preheat to 350F (175C). Deep-fry the fish in
batches in the hot oil 2 to 3 minutes until
golden-brown. Drain on paper towels. Serve
hot with lemon slices.

Makes 4 servings.

Note: The fish are eaten whole so it is necessary to choose only those which are small
enough not to require cleaning.

3 pounds mussels in their shells
1 garlic clove, chopped
1/4 cup water
1 medium-size fennel bulb
1 small onion, sliced
Salt and freshly ground pepper
1/3 cup extra-virgin olive oil
Juice of 1 lemon

Scrub mussels, rinse thoroughly and remove
beards. Discard any that do not close when
tapped firmly. Put mussels into a large saucepan with the garlic and water. Cover and
cook on high heat about 5 minutes until
shells open.

Drain and reserve 2 tablespoons of the cooking liquid. Discard any unopened mussels.
Cool mussels. Trim fennel, reserving any
feathery tops to garnish. Cut fennel bulb into
matchsticks. Place in a serving dish with
onion.

Remove and discard shells from most of the
mussels leaving about 12 to 16 mussels in
shells; reserve mussels in shells for garnish.
Add shelled mussels to serving dish with the
reserved cooking liquid. Season with salt and
freshly ground pepper. Drizzle olive oil and
lemon juice over mussels and toss to mix.
Serve sprinkled with the chopped fennel tops
and garnished with the mussels in shells.

Makes 4 to 6 servings.

STUFFED MUSSELS

MINTY SEAFOOD SALAD

3 pounds large mussels in their shells
1/3 cup dry white wine
1/2 cup fresh bread crumbs
1/3 cup olive oil
3 tablespoons chopped Italian parsley
1 tablespoon finely chopped oregano or 1 teaspoon
   dried leaf oregano
2 garlic cloves, crushed
Salt and freshly ground pepper
Lemon slices and Italian parsley leaves to garnish

Scrub mussels and remove beards. Discard
any that do not close when tapped firmly. Put
in a large saucepan with white wine.

Cover and boil 4 to 5 minutes, until shells
open. Strain, reserving liquid. Discard any
unopened mussels. Remove and discard half
of each shell leaving mussels on remaining
halves. Mix together bread crumbs, half of
the olive oil, the herbs, garlic, salt and
pepper. If mixture is dry add a little of the
reserved mussel juice to moisten.

Preheat broiler. Divide bread crumb mixture
among mussels and arrange on baking sheets.
Sprinkle with remaining olive oil and cook
under medium-hot broiler 1 to 2 minutes
until the crumb mixture is crisp and golden.
Serve hot garnished with lemon slices and
parsley leaves.

Makes 4 to 6 servings.

2/3 cup dry white wine
1 shallot, chopped
5 peppercorns
1/3 cup water
1 pound shelled scallops, fresh or frozen and thawed
1 pound cooked large shrimp
4 celery stalks
2 medium-size carrots
About 16 mint leaves
1/2 teaspoon finely grated lemon peel
DRESSING:
Juice of 2 lemons
1/2 cup extra-virgin olive oil
1 tablespoon white wine vinegar
2 tablespoons chopped Italian parsley
Salt and freshly ground pepper

Put white wine, shallot, peppercorns and
water in a shallow pan. Heat until boiling
then add scallops. Reduce heat and poach 5
to 6 minutes, until scallops are just firm and
opaque. Using a slotted spoon transfer scallops to paper towels to drain and cool.
Discard cooking liquid. Slice scallops in half
horizontally. Put in a serving dish. Peel
shrimp and add to dish.

Cut celery and carrots into thin matchsticks
and add to seafood with mint leaves and
lemon peel. Toss lightly to mix. To make
dressing, mix ingredients together in a small
bowl or put in a jar with a tight-fitting lid and
shake until blended. Pour over salad and toss.
Cover and refrigerate 30 minutes before
serving.

Makes 4 to 6 servings.

SQUID SALAD

1 pound small or medium-size squid
1-1/4 cups dry white wine
1 shallot, chopped
Strip of lemon peel
1 garlic clove, chopped
1 red onion, chopped
1/4 cup chopped mixed fresh herbs such as basil,
   tarragon and Italian parsley
Fresh herb sprigs to garnish
DRESSING:
5 tablespoons extra-virgin olive oil
2 tablespoons lemon juice
1 teaspoon balsamic vinegar
1 teaspoon Dijon-style mustard
Salt and freshly ground pepper

SCALLOPS WITH GARLIC

12 large sea scallops, on the half shell
1/4 cup extra-virgin olive oil
2 garlic cloves, chopped
2 tablespoons chopped Italian parsley
1/3 cup dry white wine
Juice of 1 lemon
Salt and freshly ground pepper
Lemon slices and parsley sprigs to garnish

Remove scallops from their shells and rinse under cold running water. Drain on paper towels. Clean 6 scallop shells thoroughly and set aside in a warm oven for serving.

Clean squid. If very small leave whole, otherwise slice into rings. Put wine, shallot, lemon peel and garlic into a medium-size saucepan. Bring to a boil and boil 1 minute. Add the squid, in batches if necessary, and cook 5 to 7 minutes until firm but still tender. Using a slotted spoon, remove to a serving dish and cool.

Heat oil in a skillet. Add garlic and parsley and cook 1 minute. Reduce heat and stir in scallops. Season with salt and freshly ground pepper, cover and cook 5 minutes, stirring twice. Stir wine into pan, and cook, covered, 3 minutes. Remove lid, increase heat and cook 4 to 5 minutes to reduce liquid by half. Remove from heat.

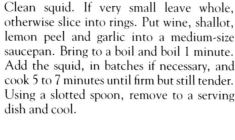

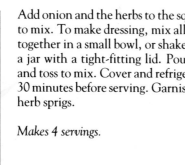

Add onion and the herbs to the squid and toss to mix. To make dressing, mix all ingredients together in a small bowl, or shake together in a jar with a tight-fitting lid. Pour over salad and toss to mix. Cover and refrigerate at least 30 minutes before serving. Garnish with fresh herb sprigs.

Makes 4 servings.

Add lemon juice to pan and stir well. Adjust seasoning and divide scallops among the reserved scallop shells. Divide cooking liquid among them. Serve immediately garnished with lemon slices and parsley sprigs.

Makes 4 to 6 servings.

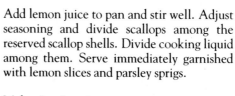

FRIED SARDINE FILLETS

1-1/2 pounds small fresh sardines, scaled
2 eggs
2 cups dried bread crumbs
1 tablespoon finely chopped oregano or 1 teaspoon
**   dried leaf oregano**
1 tablespoon finely chopped Italian parsley
Salt and freshly ground pepper
Peanut oil for deep-frying
Lemon slices to serve

Remove heads from sardines and slit each fish along stomach. Clean thoroughly. Lay each fish cut-side down on a board. Press firmly along backbone to loosen, then turn fish over and lift away bones.

Beat eggs in a shallow dish. In a separate shallow dish mix bread crumbs, herbs and seasoning.

Half-fill a deep-fryer with oil and preheat to 350F (175C). Dip each sardine fillet into beaten egg, then into bread crumb mixture to coat. Deep-fry sardines, two at a time, in the hot oil about 4 minutes until golden-brown. Drain on paper towels. Serve at once with lemon slices.

Makes 4 servings.

DEEP-FRIED SQUID & SHRIMP

8 ounces medium-size squid
12 ounces large shrimp
About 1/2 cup all-purpose flour
1 teaspoon salt
Peanut oil for deep -frying
Lemon wedges to serve
Italian parsley sprigs to garnish

Clean and prepare squid. Slice body parts into rings. Peel and devein shrimp.

Put flour in a shallow dish and season with salt and freshly ground pepper. Roll squid and shrimp in seasoned flour to coat.

Half-fill a deep-fryer or saucepan with oil and preheat to 350F (175C). Add a few pieces of fish at a time to hot oil and deep-fry about 3 minutes until golden. Using a slotted spoon transfer to paper towels to drain. Serve immediately with lemon wedges. Garnish with Italian parsley sprigs.

Makes 4 servings.

MIXED SEAFOOD SALAD

2/3 cup dry white wine
2/3 cup water
Juice of 1/2 lemon
1 shallot, chopped
8 parsley sprigs, separated into stalks and leaves
2 garlic cloves, chopped
1-1/2 pounds prepared raw seafood such as squid,
   clams, mussels and large unpeeled shrimp or shucked
   scallops
Scant 1 cup mayonnaise
1/2 teaspoon finely grated lemon peel
1 head lettuce, separated into leaves
Lemon slices to garnish
Salt and freshly ground pepper

Put wine, water, lemon juice, shallot, parsley stalks and 1 garlic clove in a large pan. Bring to a boil and boil 1 minute. Add prepared seafood according to length of cooking time of each type, starting with those that need longest cooking. (Allow 15 minutes for squid, 5 to 6 minutes for shrimp, 4 to 5 minutes for scallops, 2 to 3 minutes for mussels and clams.) Using a slotted spoon, transfer cooked pieces to a large bowl.

Strain cooking liquid into the bowl and cool. Cover and refrigerate at least 1 hour.

Chop parsley leaves with remaining garlic clove.

Put garlic and parsley into a bowl and stir in mayonnaise and lemon peel. Season with salt and freshly ground pepper. Transfer to a serving bowl.

Arrange lettuce leaves on a plate. Drain seafood and pile into center of plate. Season and garnish with lemon slices. Serve mayonnaise separately.

Makes 4 to 6 servings.

HOT ANCHOVY DIP

2 (1-3/4-oz.) cans anchovy fillets, drained and coarsely
    chopped
1-1/4 cups whipping cream
2 garlic cloves, crushed
4 tablespoons unsalted butter, diced
TO SERVE:
Cubes of crusty bread
Bread sticks
Vegetables pieces for dipping such as fennel, celery, bell
    peppers, radishes, endive and broccoli
Italian parsley leaves to garnish

TUNA-STUFFED TOMATOES

8 medium-size firm but ripe tomatoes
1 red onion, finely chopped
1 garlic clove, crushed
2 tablespoons chopped Italian parsley
2 tablespoons chopped basil or 2 teaspoons dried leaf
    basil
3 tablespoons extra-virgin olive oil
2 teaspoons red wine vinegar
1 (7-oz.) can tuna in olive oil, drained and flaked
Salt and freshly ground pepper
Mixed lettuce leaves to serve
Basil leaves to garnish

Put anchovies in a small saucepan with cream
and garlic. Bring to a boil, then reduce heat
and simmer, uncovered and stirring occasionally, 12 to 15 minutes until smooth and
thickened.

Slice tops off tomatoes and discard. Using a
teaspoon, carefully scoop out seeds and flesh
from tomatoes. Set tomatoes aside; reserve
pulp and seeds for use in sauce.

Stir in butter. Transfer to a serving dish.
Garnish with Italian parsley leaves and
serve with cubes of bread, bread sticks and
vegetables.

Makes 4 servings.

Note: Traditionally, the serving dish is kept
hot at the table like a fondue over a candle or
burner.

In a bowl, mix together onion, garlic,
parsley, basil, olive oil and vinegar. Add
tuna, salt and pepper, and stir lightly to mix.
Divide among tomatoes. Cover and refrigerate at least 1 hour before serving. Serve with
lettuce leaves. Garnish with basil leaves.

Makes 4 servings.

SHRIMP WITH MELON

12 cooked jumbo shrimp
1 small Charentais or cantaloupe melon
1 small Galia melon
Juice of 1 small lemon
Salt and freshly ground pepper
Mint leaves to garnish

Peel shrimp leaving the tail tips on, if desired.

Cut melons into thin wedges and remove skins.

Arrange shrimp and the two different colored varieties of melon on a platter or individual plates and sprinkle with lemon juice. Season with salt and freshly ground pepper. Serve garnished with mint leaves.

Makes 4 to 6 servings.

DRESSED CRAB

2 cooked crab (about 2-1/8 pounds each)
1/4 cup extra-virgin olive oil
Juice of 1 lemon
Salt and freshly ground pepper
TO GARNISH:
1 red bell pepper packed in wine vinegar, drained, cut into strips
Lemon slices
Italian parsley or fennel sprigs

Remove large claws and legs from crabs. Crack open with a small hammer and remove flesh. Flake into a bowl.

Pry open one body and remove any white meat and all the brown meat from body shells, discarding the mouth part, grey stomach sacks and feathery gills. Add all the crabmeat to the bowl. Scrub shell clean. Repeat with other crab.

Sprinkle olive oil and lemon juice over crabmeat and season with salt and freshly ground pepper. Mix together lightly with a fork. Pile meat back into crab shells and serve cold garnished with bell pepper strips, lemon slices and parsley or fennel sprigs.

Makes 4 servings.

MARINATED RAW FISH

1 pound very fresh red mullet or sardines, ready to cook
1 garlic clove, finely chopped
Juice of 2 lemons
1/2 red onion, finely chopped
1/4 teaspoon hot red pepper flakes
1/4 cup extra-virgin olive oil
Salt and freshly ground pepper
1 teaspoon chopped Italian parsley and Italian parsley
    sprig to garnish

Remove heads, tails, fins and backbones of fish. Wash fillets and pat dry. Arrange in one layer in a shallow dish.

Sprinkle with garlic and add the juice of 1-1/2 lemons. Cover and refrigerate 24 hours, turning fish once.

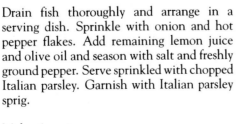
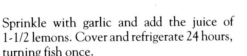
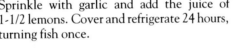

Drain fish thoroughly and arrange in a serving dish. Sprinkle with onion and hot pepper flakes. Add remaining lemon juice and olive oil and season with salt and freshly ground pepper. Serve sprinkled with chopped Italian parsley. Garnish with Italian parsley sprig.

Makes 4 servings.

Note: It is important to use fish that is very fresh as it is cooked only by the acid in the lemon juice.

TUNA SALAD

3 small carrots, thickly sliced
1-1/3 cups diced potatoes (about 8 ounces)
1 (7-oz.) can tuna in olive oil, drained and flaked
1 (1-3/4-oz.) can anchovy fillets in oil, drained and
    chopped
About 12 pitted ripe olives, halved
2 tablespoons capers in wine vinegar, drained
2 hard-cooked eggs, quartered
1/4 cup extra-virgin olive oil
Juice of 1 small lemon
1 garlic clove, crushed
Salt and freshly ground pepper
1 tablespoon chopped Italian parsley
Italian parsley sprigs to garnish

Cook carrots in a saucepan of boiling salted water 4 minutes until tender. Cook potatoes in a separate saucepan of boiling salted water about 7 minutes until tender. Drain and refresh both vegetables under cold running water, then drain and cool completely.

Put carrots, potatoes, tuna, anchovies, olives, capers and eggs into a large serving dish. Mix olive oil, lemon juice, garlic and salt and pepper together in a small bowl or put in a jar with a tight-fitting lid and shake until blended. Pour over salad, toss lightly to mix, then sprinkle with chopped Italian parsley. Garnish with Italian parsley sprigs.

Makes 4 servings.

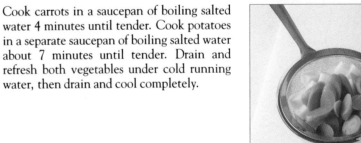

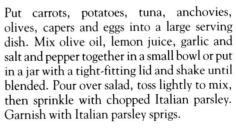

-CRABMEAT & SHRIMP TOASTS-

FRIED SHRIMP

1 cup flaked white crabmeat
3/4 cup peeled cooked shrimp
2 teaspoons lemon juice
2 tablespoons butter
1/4 cup all-purpose flour
1-1/4 cups milk
2 tablespoons marsala wine
1/2 teaspoon Dijon-style mustard
1 tablespoon chopped Italian parsley
2 tablespoons whipping cream
Salt and freshly ground pepper
4 slices crusty white bread to serve
Italian parsley sprigs and lemon slices to garnish

1 pound extra-large shrimp
1/4 cup extra-virgin olive oil
2 garlic cloves, crushed
1 small fresh green chile, seeded and sliced
2 tablespoons chopped Italian parsley
1 to 2 tablespoons anise liqueur
Salt and freshly ground pepper
Lemon wedges to garnish

Remove and discard heads and legs from shrimp.

Put crabmeat, shrimp and lemon juice into a small bowl and mix lightly. Melt butter in a small saucepan. Stir in flour and cook, stirring, 1 minute. Remove from heat, then gradually beat in milk. Return to the heat and bring to a boil, stirring constantly. Reduce heat and simmer 5 minutes, stirring frequently.

Heat oil in a large skillet. Add garlic, chile and shrimp; fry quickly 2 to 3 minutes until shrimp turn bright pink.

Stir in marsala and mustard, then remove from the heat and lightly fold in parsley, cream and the crabmeat mixture. Season with salt and freshly ground pepper. Toast bread, place on plates and top with hot mixture. Garnish with parsley sprigs and lemon slices.

Makes 4 servings.

Stir in parsley and liqueur; season with salt and freshly ground pepper. Serve at once garnished with lemon wedges.

Makes 4 servings.

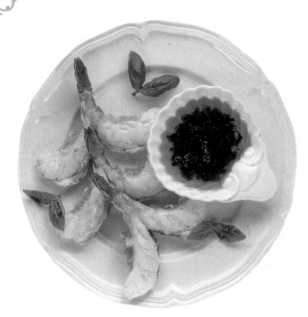

BUTTERFLIED SHRIMP

1 pound extra-large shrimp
Juice of 1 lemon
5 tablespoons extra-virgin olive oil
1/2 garlic clove, crushed
2 teaspoons sun-dried tomato paste
Pinch of red (cayenne) pepper
1 tablespoon chopped basil or 1 teaspoon dried leaf basil
Salt and freshly ground pepper
Basil sprigs to garnish

Remove and discard heads and legs from shrimp. Using sharp scissors, cut shrimp lengthwise almost in half, leaving tail end intact.

Place shrimp in a shallow dish and add half of the lemon juice and 2 tablespoons of the olive oil. Stir in garlic. Cover and marinate at least 30 minutes. Preheat broiler. Arrange shrimp in 1 layer on a rack and cook under hot broiler about 3 minutes until shrimp have curled and are bright pink.

Mix together the remaining lemon juice and the 3 tablespoons olive oil, the sun-dried tomato paste, cayenne, basil, salt and freshly ground pepper in a small bowl. Either spoon over shrimp or serve separately for dipping. Garnish shrimp with basil sprigs.

Makes 4 servings.

TUNA PATE

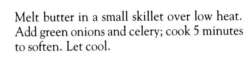

3 tablespoons butter
4 green onions, white part only, chopped
2 celery stalks, finely chopped
1 (7-oz.) can tuna in water, drained
2 tomatoes, peeled, seeded and chopped
2 tablespoons mayonnaise
1 teaspoon lemon juice
1 teaspoon white wine vinegar
Salt and freshly ground pepper
Chopped Italian parsley, parsley leaves and pitted green
    olives to garnish
Crusty bread or toast to serve

Melt butter in a small skillet over low heat. Add green onions and celery; cook 5 minutes to soften. Let cool.

Put green onion mixture in a blender or food processor with remaining ingredients, except garnish and bread. Process until fairly smooth. Transfer to a serving dish, cover and refrigerate at least 30 minutes. Garnish with chopped parsley, parsley leaves and green olives and serve with crusty bread or toast.

Makes 4 to 6 servings.

SEAFOOD PÂTÉ

1 lb. white-fish fillets
6 tablespoons butter
6 green onions, chopped
1 garlic clove, crushed
1 lb. uncooked shrimp, shelled, deveined
1/2 lb. scallops, if desired
2 tablespoons cognac or brandy
1/2 cup whipping cream
1 tablespoon lemon juice
1 teaspoon paprika
About 1/8 teaspoon red (cayenne) pepper
Salt to taste

Remove any skin from fish. Pull out any bones, then cut in chunks and set aside.

Melt butter in a large skillet over medium-low heat. Add green onions and cook, stirring, 2 minutes. Stir in garlic, fish, uncooked shrimp and scallops, if desired. Cook, stirring often, until shrimp turn pink and fish flakes. Remove from heat. Warm cognac or brandy in a small saucepan. Ignite, pour over fish mixture and let flames die down.

Stir in cream, lemon juice, paprika and red pepper. Pour cooled seafood mixture into a food processor fitted with a metal blade. Process until smooth. Season with salt. Pour mixture into 1 large or several small serving dishes, cover and refrigerate until firm. Decorate with lemon slices, dill sprigs and cooked small shrimp, if desired. Serve with crackers, melba toast or celery sticks; provide a knife for spreading.

Serves 8 to 10.

SEAFOOD TOASTS

12 slices firm-textured white bread
1/2 lb. skinned white fish fillets
1/2 lb. uncooked shrimp, shelled, deveined
2 eggs
1 tablespoon dry sherry or ginger wine
1/4 teaspoon shredded fresh gingerroot
1 tablespoon soy sauce
1/2 teaspoon salt
1 tablespoon cornstarch
Italian parsley sprigs, if desired
Vegetable oil for deep-frying

Cut a 2-3/4-inch square from center of each bread slice. Cut each square diagonally in half.

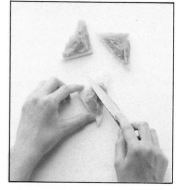

Cut fish in chunks. Place fish, shrimp, 1 egg, sherry, gingerroot, soy sauce, salt and cornstarch in a food processor fitted with a metal blade. Process to make a smooth paste. Spread seafood paste evenly over bread triangles.

Beat remaining egg; brush over seafood-topped bread. Press a parsley sprig atop each bread triangle, if desired. In a deep, heavy saucepan, heat about 2 inches of oil to 350F (180C) or until a 1-inch bread cube turns golden brown in about 65 seconds. Add seafood-topped bread, a few triangles at a time; cook until golden on all sides, turning occasionally. Drain on paper towels. Garnish with Italian parsley if desired.

Makes 24.

TARAMASALATA

2 thick slices crusty bread (about 6 oz. total)
1 (4-oz.) jar tarama
1 garlic clove, crushed
1 tablespoon grated onion
1 egg yolk
2 to 3 tablespoons lemon juice
1/2 cup olive oil
1 ripe olive
Fresh chives
Crusty bread

Trim crusts from 2 thick bread slices. Then place bread in a bowl, pour in enough cold water to cover and let soak for 10 minutes. Squeeze out excess water.

Place soaked, squeezed bread in a food processor fitted with a metal blade. Process to crumb bread evenly. Remove crumbs from work bowl; add tarama, garlic and onion. Process until thoroughly mixed. With motor running, gradually add bread crumbs, processing until mixture is smooth. Add egg yolk and 1 tablespoon lemon juice; process until blended.

With motor running, gradually pour in oil, processing until mixture is very creamy. Season with 1 to 2 tablespoons lemon juice, according to taste. Cover and refrigerate until serving time. To serve, pour in a serving bowl and garnish with olive; accompany with crusty bread for dipping.

Makes 8 to 10 servings.

SALMON MOUSSE

1 tender cucumber without too many seeds
1 (15-1/2-oz.) can red salmon
1 tablespoon unflavored gelatin
1/2 cup cold water
1/2 teaspoon dry mustard
2 tablespoons distilled white vinegar
1 teaspoon paprika
1/2 pint whipping cream (1 cup)
Melba toast or rye wafers

Trim the cucumber ends. Thinly slice lengthwise. Line a long, narrow 2-cup loaf pan with cucumber slices.

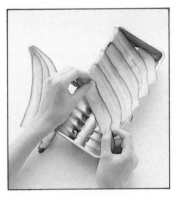

Drain salmon. Discard skin and bones, then place salmon in a food pricessor fitted with a metal blade. Process until smooth. In a small saucepan, soften gelatin in cold water; then place over low heat and stir until gelatin is dissolved. Pour gelatin over puréed salmon; add mustard, vinegar and paprika. Process until smoothly blended. With motor running, pour in cream, processing only until well mixed.

Pour into cucumber-lined pan, cover and refrigerate until set. To serve, dip pan in hot water up to rim for a couple of seconds. Invert onto a platter and lift off pan. Cut in slices; accompany with melba toast or rye wafers. Place atop melba toast to serve.

Makes 4 to 6 servings.

SALMON PUFFS

1/2 cup water
1/2 teaspoon salt
1/4 cup butter, cut in pieces
1/2 cup all-purpose flour
1/4 cup shredded Cheddar cheese (1 oz.)
2 eggs
1 (7-1/2-oz.) can red salmon
2 tablespoons mayonnaise
1 tablespoon sliced pimento-stuffed green olives
Red and black caviar, if desired

Preheat oven to 400F (200C). Grease 2 baking sheets. Sift flour. In a saucepan, heat water, salt and butter until butter is melted stirring constantly. Bring mixture to a full boil.

Add flour all at once. Stir over low heat about 1 minute or until mixture leaves sides of pan and forms a ball. Remove from heat, stir in cheese and cool slightly. Beat in eggs, 1 at a time, beating until smooth after each addition.

Drop batter by teaspoonfuls onto greased baking sheets. Bake about 20 minutes or until puffy and golden. Remove from baking sheets; cool on racks. Cut each puff in half; scoop out any soft centers. Drain salmon. Discard skin and bones. Place salmon in a bowl; flake with a fork and mix in mayonnaise and olives. Fill puffs with salmon mixture; if desired, dip in caviar. Serve immediately.

Makes about 25.

CRISPY ALMOND SQUID

1 lb. cleaned squid bodies (mantles)
1/2 cup all-purpose flour
Salt and pepper to taste
2 eggs
1 cup fine dry bread crumbs
1/2 cup finely chopped unblanched almonds
Vegetable oil for deep-frying

Slice squid bodies crosswise into rings.

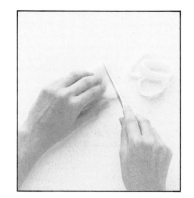

Combine flour, salt and pepper in a shallow dish. In another shallow dish beat eggs to blend well. On a sheet of wax paper mix bread crumbs and almonds. Roll squid in flour mixture, a few pieces at a time; dip in beaten eggs, then roll in crumb mixture to coat well. Arrange crumb-coated squid in a single layer on a baking sheet or flat platter. Cover and refrigerate until ready to cook.

To cook, in a deep, heavy saucepan, heat about 2 inches of oil to 375F (190C) or until a 1-inch bread cube turns golden brown in about 50 seconds. Add squid, a few pieces at a time, and cook just until golden on all sides; do not overcook or squid will toughen. Remove from oil with a slotted spoon and drain well on paper towels.

Makes 4 to 8 servings.

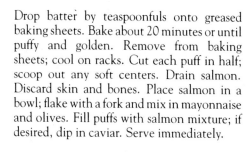

CAVIAR MOLDS

1/2 lb. black caviar, drained, rinsed
2 teaspoons unflavored gelatin
1/2 cup cold water
1-1/4 cups dairy sour cream
3 green onions, finely chopped
Quail eggs or hard-cooked hen eggs, if desired
Fresh fennel sprigs and Italian parsley

Place caviar in a bowl. In a small saucepan, soften gelatin in cold water; then place over low heat and stir until gelatin is dissolved. Stir dissolved gelatin into caviar.

Divide mixture evenly among 4 individual 1/2-cup molds or pour into a 2-cup mold. Refrigerate until set or up to 24 hours (this dish is best made no earlier than 1 day before serving). Meanwhile, in a small bowl, stir together sour cream and green onions; cover and refrigerate. If using quail eggs for garnish, boil 5 minutes, then cool and remove shells.

To serve, dip each mold up to rim in hot water; invert onto a platter. Lift off molds. If desired, garnish with lemon wedges and quail eggs or hard-cooked hen eggs. If using hen eggs, cut decorative shapes from the whites; press yolks through a sieve. Arrange egg-white shapes on molds; place the sieved yolks in the center. Serve with sour cream mixture.

Makes four 1/2-cup molds or one 2-cup mold.

HERB & GARLIC MUSSELS

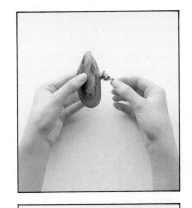

2 lbs. mussels in-the-shell
1/2 cup butter, room temperature
2 garlic cloves, crushed
2 tablespoons chopped parsley
1 tablespoon chopped chives
1 tablespoon chopped fresh dill

Scrub mussels well with a stiff brush. Pull out and discard beards. Then soak mussels several hours in cold water to cover; discard any mussels with broken shells. Drain well.

In a large saucepan, bring 2 cups water to a boil. Add as many mussels as will fit in a single layer; boil until shells open, then remove from pan. Repeat with remaining mussels, adding uncooked mussels as cooked ones are removed. Lift off and discard top shell of each mussel. Discard any mussels that do not open.

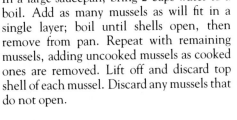

In a bowl, beat butter, garlic, parsley, chives and dill until well blended. Spread mixture evenly over mussels. Cover and refrigerate until ready to cook. To cook, preheat broiler. Arrange mussels in a broiler pan; broil until tops are lightly browned. Serve hot.

Makes about 30, depending on size of mussels.

CAVIAR CROUTONS

—OPEN SALMON SANDWICHES—

10 slices firm-textured white bread
2 tablespoons butter
2 tablespoons vegetable oil
1 to 2 teaspoons prepared horseradish, or to taste
1/2 cup dairy sour cream
3 tablespoons red salmon caviar
Small parsley sprigs, if desired

To make croutons, cut 2 shapes from each bread slice. Cut hearts with cookie or hors d'oeuvres cutters; cut diamonds with a knife. Reserve bread trimmings for breadcrumbs or other uses.

Melt butter in oil in a medium skillet. When fat is hot, add bread shapes. Cook, turning as needed, until golden on both sides. Drain on paper towels. If prepared ahead, cool; then store in an airtight container up to 24 hours. In a small bowl, stir together horseradish and sour cream.

Just before serving, spoon sour-cream mixture onto croutons and top with caviar. If desired, garnish each canapé with a parsley sprig.

Makes 20.

6 thin slices pumpernickel, light rye or dark rye bread
1/4 cup butter, room temperature
Crisp chicory or lettuce leaves, torn in small pieces
1/2 lb. thinly sliced smoked salmon
Dill sprigs and lemon twists

Using a cookie cutter, cut each bread slice into a round. Spread rounds liberally with butter.

Top each round with chicory or lettuce, then with a folded smoked-salmon slice. Garnish each sandwich with a dill sprig and a lemon twist. Serve immediately; or cover and refrigerate until ready to serve (up to 1 hour).

Makes 6.

Variation: If desired, top each sandwich with a dab of dairy sour cream flavored with chopped fresh dill and chopped capers.

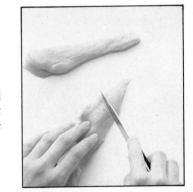

PROSCIUTTO ROULADES

2 oz. ricotta cheese (1/4 cup)
2 oz. Stilton cheese, crumbled
1 tablespoon dairy sour cream
12 very thin slices prosciutto, coppa salami or lean
    cooked ham
1 pear
Lemon juice
Lime slices and dill sprigs, if desired

In a small bowl, thoroughly blend ricotta cheese, Stilton cheese and sour cream. Spread evenly on prosciutto, salami or ham slices, spreading mixture almost to edges.

Peel, quarter and core pear, then cut each quarter lengthwise in 3 thin slices. Brush slices lightly with lemon juice to prevent darkening. Place a pear slice on each cheese-topped prosciutto slice.

Roll up prosciutto slices, cover and refrigerate until ready to serve. Garnish with lime slice and dill sprig, if desired.

Makes 12.

Variation: Substitute an apple or fresh figs for the pear. Peel and slice figs before using.

YAKITORI

1/2 lb. skinned, boned chicken breast
6 green onions
2 tablespoons sake
2 tablespoons light soy sauce
1/2 teaspoon grated fresh gingerroot
2 teaspoons sugar

Cut chicken in small cubes. Trim roots and any wilted leaves from green onions, then cut each onion in 1-1/2-inch lengths, using some tops.

Thread chicken alternatively with green onions on 6 bamboo skewers.

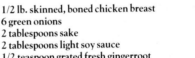

Preheat broiler. In a small saucepan, heat sake; stir in soy sauce, gingerroot and sugar. Remove from heat. Place skewers in a broiler pan; cover any exposed bamboo at ends of skewers with foil. Brush sake mixture over skewers. Broil, brushing often with marinade and turning occasionally, about 6 minutes, or until chicken is no longer pink in center; cut to test. Serve hot.

Makes 6.

STUFFED ONIONS

4 large onions
8 ounces ground veal
2 slices bacon, finely chopped
1/3 cup shredded provolone cheese
1 or 2 garlic cloves, crushed
1 tablespoon sun-dried tomato paste
1 tablespoon finely chopped Italian parsley
1 tablespoon chopped oregano or 1 teaspoon dried leaf oregano
1 small egg, beaten
Salt and freshly ground pepper
Fresh Italian parsley sprigs or oregano sprigs to garnish

Grease a baking dish. Peel onions and place in a large saucepan, cover with water and bring to a boil. Cook 25 to 30 minutes until just tender. Drain and cool slightly. Preheat oven to 400F (205C). Cut onions in half horizontally. Using a teaspoon, carefully remove centers of onions, leaving shells about 3 layers thick. Use pieces from the centers to cover any holes in the bottoms; discard remaining centers.

Mix together remaining ingredients, except garnish, in a small bowl. Divide among onion shells and arrange them in the baking dish. Bake in preheated oven 40 to 45 minutes until filling is cooked through. Serve hot garnished with Italian parsley or oregano sprigs.

Makes 4 servings.

POLLO FRITTO

1 pound chicken breast and thigh meat
3 tablespoons olive oil
Juice of 1/2 lemon
1 garlic clove, crushed
About 1/2 cup all-purpose flour
2 eggs, beaten
2 cups dried bread crumbs
1 teaspoon paprika
Salt and freshly ground pepper
Peanut oil or light olive oil for deep-frying
Lemon wedges and Italian parsley leaves to garnish

Cut chicken into 2-inch pieces and place in a shallow dish. Add the 3 tablespoons olive oil, lemon juice and garlic and stir well. Cover and marinate at least 1 hour. Put flour into a shallow dish. Put eggs into a second shallow dish, and mix together bread crumbs, paprika and seasoning in a third dish. Drain chicken. Coat a few pieces at a time first in flour, then eggs, then in seasoned bread crumb mixture.

Half-fill a deep-fat fryer with oil, and preheat to 350F (175C). Deep-fry coated chicken pieces, in batches, about 3 minutes, turning once, until crisp and golden. Serve hot garnished with lemon wedges and parsley leaves.

Makes 4 servings.

BRESAOLA SALAD

VENETIAN CHICKEN SALAD

16 slices bresaola
Mixed lettuce leaves
4 large fresh basil leaves, shredded
DRESSING:
3 tablespoons extra-virgin olive oil
1/4 teaspoon finely grated lemon peel
Juice of 1/2 lemon
Salt and freshly ground pepper
Basil leaves and lemon slices to garnish

1/4 cup raisins
Juice of 1 orange
1/3 cup pine nuts
1 pound cooked chicken breast, cut into strips
Small pinch of ground cloves
1/3 cup extra-virgin olive oil
1 tablespoon white wine vinegar
1 to 2 teaspoons balsamic vinegar
Salt and freshly ground pepper
Mixed lettuce leaves to serve

Heat raisins and orange juice to boiling in a small saucepan. Remove from heat. Let stand 20 minutes. Drain and set aside raisins; discard liquid.

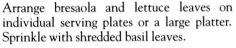

Arrange bresaola and lettuce leaves on individual serving plates or a large platter. Sprinkle with shredded basil leaves.

Put pine nuts into a small saucepan or skillet, without oil; place over medium heat and stir 3 minutes until golden.

In a small bowl, mix together olive oil, lemon peel and lemon juice and spoon over bresaola and lettuce. Season with salt and freshly ground pepper. Garnish with basil leaves and lemon slices.

Makes 4 servings.

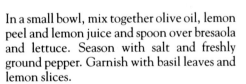

Put pine nuts and all other ingredients, except lettuce, into a bowl and toss well to mix. Cover and refrigerate 30 minutes. Serve with lettuce leaves.

Makes 4 to 6 servings.

PROSCIUTTO WITH FIGS

BRESAOLA & CHEESE ROLLS

12 paper-thin slices prosciutto
4 to 6 ripe figs
Fresh Italian parsley leaves or mint sprigs to garnish

4 ounces dolcelatte cheese
2 ounces mascarpone cheese
Salt and freshly ground pepper
12 thin slices bresaola
Mixed lettuce leaves
Juice of 1 lemon
3 tablespoons extra-virgin olive oil
Lemon slices to garnish

In a small bowl mix together dolcelatte and mascarpone cheeses until well blended. Season with salt and freshly ground pepper.

Arrange prosciutto on a platter or individual plates.

Lay bresaola slices flat on a board. Divide mixture among slices and roll up.

Halve figs lengthwise, then cut into quarters, and arrange beside ham. Serve garnished with parsley leaves or mint sprigs.

Makes 4 servings.

Arrange lettuce leaves on a platter or individual plates and place the bresaola rolls on top. Sprinkle with lemon juice and olive oil and a little more pepper. Serve garnished with lemon slices.

Makes 4 servings.

CARPACCIO

ITALIAN MEAT PLATTER

1 (10-oz.) piece beef tenderloin
1 (3-oz.) piece Parmesan cheese, thinly sliced
3 cups thinly sliced button mushrooms (8 ounces)
Leaves from about 8 Italian parsley sprigs
DRESSING:
1/2 cup extra-virgin olive oil
Juice of 2 lemons
1 garlic clove, chopped
Salt and freshly ground pepper

Put beef in freezer 30 minutes. Using a very sharp knife, cut beef into wafer-thin slices.

Lay beef slices in the center of a large serving plate and arrange Parmesan slices, mushrooms and parsley around edge.

To make dressing, whisk ingredients together in a small bowl or put in a jar with a tight-fitting lid and shake until thoroughly blended. Pour over beef, cheese, mushrooms and parsley.

Makes 6 servings.

4 ounces thinly sliced mixed salamis
2 ounces thinly sliced mortadella
2 ounces thinly sliced prosciutto or coppa
2 ounces thinly sliced bresaola
2 large pickles
1 small bunch radishes, trimmed
6 ounces cherry tomatoes
3/4 cup ripe olives or green olives
Lettuce leaves
Italian parsley leaves to garnish
DRESSING:
5 tablespoons extra-virgin olive oil
2 tablespoons lemon juice
1 tablespoon red wine vinegar
1 teaspoon Dijon-style mustard
Salt and freshly ground pepper

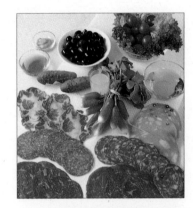

Arrange meats on a large platter. Thinly slice pickles on the diagonal and add to platter with radishes, tomatoes, olives and lettuce leaves.

To make dressing, mix all ingredients together in a small bowl and serve with meat platter. Garnish with parsley leaves.

Makes 6 to 8 servings.

Note: The selection of meats can be varied to include your favorites. Serve with crusty bread, bread rolls or bread sticks.

VEAL & SPINACH TERRINE

1 pound fresh spinach
1 pound ground veal
4 slices bacon, finely chopped
3/4 cup shredded provolone cheese (3 ounces)
1/2 cup fresh bread crumbs
1 tablespoon chopped Italian parsley
2 eggs, beaten
Salt and freshly ground pepper
Italian parsley sprigs to garnish

PORK & LIVER PATE

12 ounces bacon slices
8 ounces lean pork, chopped
8 ounces pork liver, chopped
8 ounces pork sausage
1 small onion, finely chopped
2 garlic cloves, chopped
1 tablespoon chopped thyme
1 tablespoon chopped oregano
3 tablespoons marsala wine
Salt and freshly ground pepper
Thyme and oregano sprigs to garnish

Preheat oven to 325F (165C). Grease an 8″ × 4″ loaf pan. Lay bacon slices flat on a board and stretch using the back of a knife.

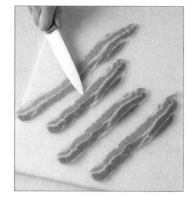

Preheat oven to 325F (165C). Grease and line bottom of a 9″ × 5″ loaf pan with waxed paper. Rinse spinach thoroughly; do not dry. Cook in a large saucepan without additional water about 2 minutes until wilted. Transfer to a colander and press out excess water using a wooden spoon. Chop finely.

Line the loaf pan, with the bacon slices, reserving a few slices to cover the top. Place pork in a blender or food processor and process until finely chopped. Add remaining ingredients and process briefly until well blended but not smooth. Put pork mixture into loaf pan, smooth top and cover with reserved bacon. Cover tightly with oiled foil.

In a large bowl, mix together spinach and remaining ingredients, except parsley sprigs. Spoon into the loaf pan and smooth the top Cover with oiled foil and cook in preheated oven 1 to 1-1/4 hours until firm. Remove from oven, cool slightly, then refrigerate in pan until cold. Turn out and slice; garnish with parsley sprigs.

Makes 6 servings.

Place loaf pan in a roasting pan half-filled with boiling water. Cook in preheated oven 1-1/2 to 1-3/4 hours until firm. Remove foil. Cover pate with waxed paper, then put a plate or board and a heavy weight on top; refrigerate overnight before turning out. Slice to serve and garnish with herb sprigs.

Makes 6 to 8 servings.

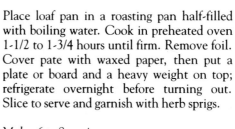

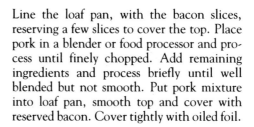

HAM CRESCENTS

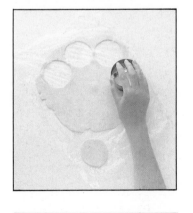

4 oz. cream cheese, room temperature
1/2 cup butter, room temperature
1 cup all-purpose flour
1/2 lb. cooked ham, cut in chunks
1 teaspoon prepared hot mustard
2 tablespoons dairy sour cream
1 egg, beaten

In a bowl, beat cream cheese and butter until light and creamy. Blend in flour. Turn out dough onto a floured work surface; knead lightly. Wrap in plastic wrap and refrigerate until firm enough to handle. Meanwhile, place ham in a food processor fitted with a metal blade; process until finely minced. (Or mince ham with a knife.) Turn ham into a bowl and mix in mustard and sour cream. Cover and refrigerate until ready to use.

On a well-floured board, roll out pastry thinly. (Or dust 2 sheets of plastic wrap with flour; roll out pastry between floured sheets of plastic wrap.) Cut rolled-out dough into 3-inch rounds.

Preheat oven to 400F (200C). Place 1 heaping teaspoon of filling on each pastry round. Brush edges of each round with egg; fold pastry rounds in half over filling. Press edges with a fork to seal. Prick each pastry with tip of a sharp knife to allow steam to escape. Arrange pastries on baking sheets; bake 10 to 15 minutes or until golden. Serve hot.

Makes 20 to 24.

CHICKEN & GRAPE SALAD

1 pound cooked chicken breasts
1-1/4 cups walnut halves
1 cup seedless green grapes, halved
16 stuffed green olives, sliced
3 green onions, sliced
Salt and freshly ground pepper
1 head romaine lettuce, separated into leaves
DRESSING:
2/3 cup mayonnaise
1 garlic clove, chopped
1 teaspoon paprika
2 tablespoons chopped Italian parsley
Few drops of hot pepper sauce
2 tablespoons milk

Cut chicken into thin strips, and place in a bowl with walnuts, grapes, olives and green onions. Season with salt and freshly ground pepper.

To make dressing, mix all ingredients together in a small bowl. Pour over salad and toss gently to mix. Arrange lettuce on a serving plate. Pile chicken salad in center and serve at once.

Makes 4 to 6 servings.

ITALIAN SAUSAGES & LENTILS

2 cups green lentils
2 tablespoons extra-virgin olive oil
2 slices bacon, chopped
1 onion, finely chopped
2 garlic cloves, crushed
2 celery stalks, finely chopped
Salt and freshly ground pepper
4 to 6 fresh spicy Italian pork sausages
Chopped Italian parsley and parsley sprigs to garnish

Put lentils in a bowl, cover with cold water and soak 2 hours. Drain.

Heat 1 tablespoon of the oil in a large sauce-pan. Add bacon, onion, garlic and celery; cook 3 to 4 minutes until beginning to brown. Add lentils and enough water to just cover. Bring to a boil, reduce heat and simmer 25 minutes until lentils are tender, adding a little more water if necessary. Season with salt and freshly ground pepper.

Meanwhile, in a skillet, fry sausages in the remaining 1 tablespoon oil about 10 minutes, turning occasionally, until evenly browned. Thickly slice sausages. Spoon lentils onto a warmed serving plate, place sausage slices on top and sprinkle with chopped parsley and garnish with parsley sprigs.

Makes 4 to 6 servings.

SAUTEED LAMB KIDNEYS

12 lamb kidneys
2 tablespoons butter
1 tablespoon olive oil
2 garlic cloves, crushed
1 small onion, finely chopped
1 teaspoon whole-grain mustard
1/4 cup marsala wine
Salt and freshly ground pepper
Hot toasted bread to serve
Chopped Italian parsley and parsley sprigs to garnish

Remove and discard the thin membrane surrounding kidneys. Cut each in half. Using kitchen scissors, snip out white cores.

Heat butter and oil in a large skillet. Add garlic and onion and saute 3 minutes until just softened. Add kidneys and cook over high heat, stirring, 2 to 3 minutes until browned but still tender.

Stir mustard and marsala into pan and cook 1 minute. Season with salt and freshly ground pepper. Serve on hot toasted bread and sprinkle with chopped Italian parsley and garnish with parsley sprigs.

Makes 4 to 6 servings.

FRITTO MISTO

About 3/4 cup all-purpose flour
Salt and freshly ground pepper
2 eggs, beaten
About 2 cups dry bread crumbs
4 lamb kidneys, halved and cored
8 ounces calves' liver, cut into strips
8 ounces fresh spicy Italian sausages, cut into bite-size
   pieces
1 small eggplant, sliced
2 medium-size zucchini, thickly sliced
Vegetable oil for deep-frying
Italian parsley sprigs to garnish

Put flour into a shallow dish; season with salt and freshly ground pepper. Put eggs into a second shallow dish and bread crumbs into a third dish. Dip kidneys, liver, sausages, eggplant and zucchini first in seasoned flour, then in eggs and finally in bread crumbs to coat evenly.

Half-fill a deep-fat fryer with oil. Preheat to 350F (175C). Deep-fry meats and vegetables, in batches, 2 to 4 minutes, turning once, until crisp and golden. Using a slotted spoon, transfer to paper towels to drain. Serve hot garnished with parsley sprigs.

Makes 6 to 8 servings.

CHICKEN LIVER TOASTS

3 tablespoons olive oil
1 celery stalk, finely chopped
2 garlic cloves, crushed
8 ounces chicken livers, chopped
1 teaspoon chopped fresh sage
1/4 cup marsala wine
2 anchovy fillets canned in oil, drained
1 tablespoon capers in wine vinegar, drained
Freshly ground pepper
1 medium-size loaf French bread
Capers and fresh sage leaves to garnish

Preheat oven to 375F (190C). Heat oil in a large skillet. Add celery and garlic and cook 2 minutes to soften.

Add chicken livers and fry over high heat about 3 minutes, stirring occasionally, until crisp and brown on outside but still pink inside. Using a wooden spoon, stir in sage and marsala, scraping up all the cooking juices. Transfer to a blender or food processor and add anchovy fillets and capers. Season with freshly ground pepper and process until fairly smooth. Transfer to a warmed plate, cover and place over a saucepan of hot water to keep warm.

Cut bread diagonally into thick slices and lay on a baking sheet. Bake in preheated oven 6 to 7 minutes until golden. Serve the chicken liver paste on the baked bread, and garnish with capers and sage leaves.

Makes 6 to 8 servings.

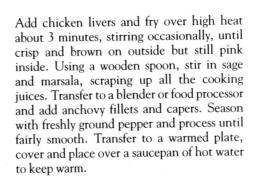

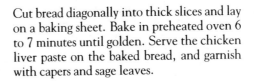

—CHICKEN WITH GREEN SAUCE—

—BRANDIED LIVER PATE—

1 pound cooked chicken breasts
Mixed lettuce leaves
Italian parsley sprigs to garnish
SAUCE:
1 bunch Italian parsley
8 basil sprigs
1 (1-3/4-oz.) can anchovy fillets in oil, drained
1 shallot, chopped
2 garlic cloves, crushed
3 tablespoons white wine vinegar
1 teaspoon Dijon-style mustard
1/4 cup fresh bread crumbs
Freshly ground pepper
1/2 cup extra-virgin olive oil

8 ounces calves' liver
8 ounces chicken livers
1/2 cup butter
Rosemary sprig
1 bay leaf
5 tablespoons brandy
Salt and freshly ground pepper
Rosemary sprigs to garnish

Discard any veins from livers. Dice calves' liver, and cut chicken livers in half.

To make sauce, using a blender or food processor, process all sauce ingredients, except olive oil, to a smooth paste. With motor running, slowly pour in oil to make a thick but pourable consistency.

Melt 2 tablespoons of the butter in a large skillet, add rosemary, bay leaf and chicken livers and cook over high heat 3 minutes, stirring occasionally, until crisp on the outside but still pink inside. Remove to a blender or food processor and set aside. Add calves' liver to the pan and cook over high heat about 3 minutes. Add to chicken livers. Using a wooden spoon, stir 2 tablespoons of the brandy into pan scraping up the cooking juices.

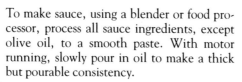

Slice the chicken and arrange with lettuce leaves on a serving plate or individual plates. Pour sauce over and around the chicken. Garnish with parsley sprigs.

Makes 4 to 6 servings.

Discard herbs from pan, then pour cooking juices into the blender or food processor; process until smooth. Transfer to a bowl, and cool. Beat in remaining butter and brandy. Season with salt and freshly ground pepper. Transfer to a serving dish, cover and refrigerate a few hours until firm. Serve garnished with rosemary sprigs.

Makes 4 servings.

CHINESE DUMPLINGS

1 (8-oz.) can bamboo shoots, drained
4 green onions
1/2 lb. lean ground pork
1/2 teaspoon grated fresh gingerroot
1 teaspoon salt
1 egg white
2 teaspoons soy sauce
About 20 won-ton skins
Tomato roses and Italian parsley, if desired
Plum sauce or chili sauce

Finely chop the drained bamboo shoots and the green onions. In a bowl, combine bamboo shoots, green onions, pork, gingerroot, salt, egg white and soy sauce. Work with won-ton skins a few at a time, keeping remaining skins covered with damp paper towels or plastic wrap to prevent drying.

To shape each dumpling, place a heaping teaspoon of filling on 1 won-ton skin. Bring sides of skin up around filling; squeeze together so it looks like a money pouch.

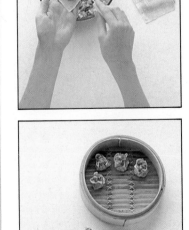

To cook, arrange dumplings slightly apart in a bamboo steaming basket. Steam over boiling water 20 minutes. Arrange on a platter with tomato roses and Italian parsley, if desired. Serve with plum sauce or chili sauce for dipping.

Makes about 20.

SPICY PORK ROLLS

1/2 lb. pork tenderloin
6 or 7 green onions
1 garlic clove, crushed
1 tablespoon dark soy sauce
1 tablespoon honey
1 tablespoon vegetable oil
1 tablespoon hoisin sauce
1 teaspoon grated fresh gingerroot

Trim any excess fat from pork, then cut crosswise in 20 slices.

Flatten meat slices with a knife. Trim roots and any wilted leaves from green onions, then cut each onion in 3 or 4 pieces.

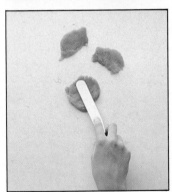

Roll each meat slice around 1 green onion piece. (There's no need to fasten rolls closed – moisture in meat will keep them from coming open.) Preheat oven to 400F (200C). In a shallow baking dish, stir together garlic, soy sauce, honey, oil, hoisin sauce and gingerroot. Place pork rolls in soy mixture and turn to coat. If preparing ahead, cover and refrigerate. Bake, uncovered, 10 to 15 minutes or until meat is no longer pink in center; cut to test. During baking, baste rolls frequently with sauce. Serve hot or warm.

Makes 20.

SALAMI CRESCENTS

1 (17-1/4-oz.) pkg. frozen puff pastry, thawed
2 tablespoons dairy sour cream
1 teaspoon prepared hot mustard
16 slices mettwurst salami
8 slices Swiss cheese, room temperature
1 egg, beaten

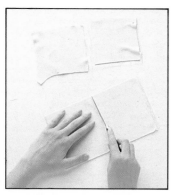

Unfold pastry sheets. On a lightly floured board, roll out each sheet of pastry to a 14-inch square. Cut each square in quarters, making a total of eight 7-inch squares.

Preheat oven to 400F (200C). In a small bowl, mix sour cream and mustard. Spread evenly over pastry squares, spreading almost to edges of pastry. Cut each salami slice in half; cut each cheese slice diagonally in half. Arrange salami and cheese on pastry; cut each pastry square diagonally in half to make 2 triangles, then cut into quarters.

Starting from wide side, roll up each pastry triangle. Arrange on baking sheets, points underneath; bend pastries gently into crescent shapes. Brush with egg. Bake 10 to 15 minutes until golden.

Makes 32.

LIVERWURST CANAPÉS

1 (about 12-inch-long) crusty baguette
3 tablespoons olive oil
2 tablespoons butter, melted
1 small garlic clove, crushed
6 thin slices Swiss cheese
1/2 lb. smoked liverwurst
Pickled sweet gherkins

Preheat oven to 400F (200C). Cut baguette in 1/2-inch-thick slices.

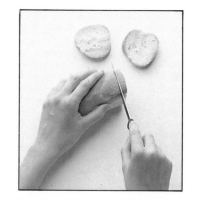

Stir together oil, melted butter and garlic; brush on both sides of bread slices. Arrange in a single layer in a baking dish. Bake 10 minutes or until bread is golden and crisp around edges. Meanwhile, cut each cheese slice in quarters; set aside. In a bowl, beat liverwurst until softened.

Spread liverwurst evenly on each slice of hot toast. Top each slice with 1 piece of cheese; return to oven and bake 5 to 10 minutes longer or until cheese is melted. Garnish each canapé with a pickled sweet gherkin and serve hot.

Makes about 24.

SATAY SAUSAGE ROLLS

1 tablespoon vegetable oil
1 onion, finely chopped
1 tablespoon dark soy sauce
2 teaspoons lemon juice
2 garlic cloves, crushed
Hot sauce to taste
3 eggs
1-1/2 lbs. pork sausagemeat
3 sheets frozen puff pastry (1-1/2 x 17-1/4-oz. pkg.)
   thawed

Heat oil in a medium saucepan over a low heat. Add onion; cook until soft, stirring occasionally. Stir in soy sauce, lemon juice, garlic and sauce.

In a large bowl, thoroughly mix onion mixture, 2 eggs and sausage. Set aside. Preheat oven to 400F (200C). Unfold pastry sheets. Place on a lightly floured board and roll out slightly to make a 22″ x 10″ rectangle. Cut rectangle in two 11″ x 10″ strips; cut each strip in half lengthwise again to make four 5-1/2″ x 10″ strips.

Spoon 1/4 of sausage mixture down center of each pastry strip. Beat remaining egg; brush over edges of pastry strips. Fold pastry over filling; press to seal. Slash top of each pastry roll; cut each roll in 1- to 1-1/2-inch lengths. Arrange on baking sheets; bake about 20 minutes or until golden. Serve hot with spicy sauce.

Makes about 40.

LIVERWURST BALLS

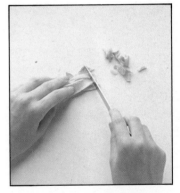

2 bacon slices
1 small onion, finely chopped
1/2 lb. liverwurst
2 tablespoons brandy or orange-flavored liqueur
About 1 cup chopped parsley
Orange slices and orange peel strips, if desired

Cut the bacon slices in fine dice. In a skillet, cook bacon over low heat, stirring, until it begins to turn crisp. Remove bacon from pan. Add onion to dripping in pan; cook over low heat, stirring until soft.

In a large bowl, combine bacon, onion and liverwurst; mix well. Warm brandy or liqueur in a small saucepan. Carefully ignite; pour over liverwurst mixture and let flame die down. Mix well. Cover and refrigerate until firm.

Spread parsley on a sheet of waxed paper. Roll chilled liverwurst mixture into balls, a heaping teaspoonful at a time then roll in parsley to coat well. Arrange on a plate, cover and refrigerate until ready to serve. If desired, garnish with orange slices and orange peel strips.

Makes 12 to 15.

BARBECUED CSABAI

2 pairs hot or original (mild) csabai sausage (*not* csabai salami, which is much harder)

Cut csabai into about 3-inch lengths and peel off skin.

Then split each piece of csabai in half lengthwise. Cover and refrigerate until ready to cook.

To cook, arrange sausage pieces, cut sides down, on a lightly greased grill about 4 inches above a solid bed of glowing coals. (Or cook in a large skillet over medium heat.) Cook, turning as needed, until browned on all sides. Cut in chunks and serve hot.

Makes 40 to 60 pieces.

Tip: This appetizer is an ideal beginning for a barbecue meal – not only do the sausages taste delicious, but their flavor penetrates the meats cooked for the main course. If you don't want to barbecue the sausage, you may broil or pan-fry it.

PIROSHKI WITH THYME

2 oz. fresh yeast
2 tablespoons sugar
3/4 cup warm milk 110F (45C)
3 cups all-purpose flour
2 teaspoons salt
3/4 cup butter
3 large onions, chopped
1/2 lb. bacon slices, finely chopped
1 teaspoon pepper
2 tablespoons fresh thyme leaves
1 egg beaten

Cream yeast with sugar. Stir in milk.

In a bowl, stir together flour and salt. Stir in yeast mixture and 1/2 cup melted butter. Beat to mix well; then beat vigorously about 3 minutes to make a smooth batter. Cover with plastic wrap and let rise in a warm place about 1 hour or until doubled. Melt remaining 1/4 cup butter in a large skillet. Add onions and cook until soft and golden, sitrring frequently; cool. Stir in bacon, pepper and thyme.

Punch down dough. Turn out onto a lightly floured board and knead briefly, then divide into 35 to 40 equal portions. Wrap a spoonful of filling in each portion of dough. Grease 2 or 3 baking sheets; arrange piroshki on baking sheets and let rise in a warm place 15 minutes. Brush piroshki with egg. Preheat oven to 450F (230C). Bake 10 to 15 minutes or until golden.

Makes 35 to 40.

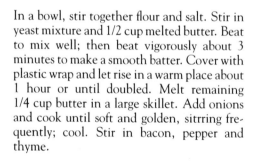

CHICKEN & SAUSAGE ROLLS

RUMAKI

1 lb. skinned, boned chicken breasts
Salt and pepper to taste
2 or 3 pepperoni sausages
12 green beans, ends and strings removed
6 sheets filo pastry
1/2 cup butter, melted

Slice the chicken in half to make 2 thin breasts; place between sheets of plastic wrap and pound with a flat-surfaced mallet to make a thin, even layer. Sprinkle with salt and pepper. Divide pounded chicken into 6 portions.

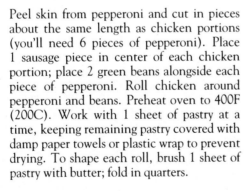

Peel skin from pepperoni and cut in pieces about the same length as chicken portions (you'll need 6 pieces of pepperoni). Place 1 sausage piece in center of each chicken portion; place 2 green beans alongside each piece of pepperoni. Roll chicken around pepperoni and beans. Preheat oven to 400F (200C). Work with 1 sheet of pastry at a time, keeping remaining pastry covered with damp paper towels or plastic wrap to prevent drying. To shape each roll, brush 1 sheet of pastry with butter; fold in quarters.

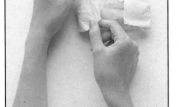

Place 1 chicken roll in center of folded pastry sheet; tuck in sides and roll up. Place rolls in shallow-rimmed baking pan; brush with remaining melted butter. Bake 15 to 20 minutes or until golden and crisp. Cut each roll in about 5 chunks; serve hot.

Makes 30.

1 lb. chicken livers
2 tablespoons vegetable oil
1 tablespoon soy sauce
1 tablespoon dry sherry
Squeeze of lemon juice
1 garlic clove, crushed
About 12 bacon slices
10 canned water chestnuts, drained, sliced

Rinse chicken livers, pat dry and cut each liver in half. Then cut out any dark spots, large veins and membranes. Heat oil in a large skillet over medium-low heat. Add livers, a portion at a time; cook, turning constantly, just until livers are no longer red on outside.

Remove skillet from heat. Return all livers to skillet, then mix in soy sauce, sherry, lemon juice and garlic. Cool completely. Cut each bacon slice in halves or thirds.

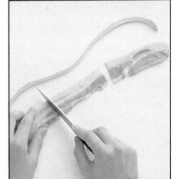

Place 1 piece of chicken liver on 1 bacon piece; top with a slice of water chestnut. Roll bacon around livers and water chestnuts; secure with a wooden pick. Repeat with remaining bacon, livers and water chestnuts. Cover and refrigerate until ready to cook. To cook, preheat broiler. Arrange rumaki in a broiler pan; broil until crisp. Serve hot.

Makes about 28.

SMOKED-BEEF TARTS

1 cup all-purpose flour
Pinch of salt
1 tablespoon grated Parmesan cheese
1/4 cup firm butter
1 egg, beaten
1 (14-oz.) can artichoke hearts, drained
1/4 lb. thinly sliced smoked beef
2 tablespoons dairy sour cream
2 teaspoons chopped fresh dill
1 red pepper, cored, seeded, cut in thin strips

In a bowl, stir together flour, salt and cheese. Cut in butter until mixture resembles coarse crumbs. Add egg all at once, stir with a fork until dough holds together. Gather into a ball, wrap and refrigerate 30 minutes.

Lightly grease about 15 small tart pans. Dust 2 sheets of plastic wrap with flour. Roll out pastry thinly between sheets of floured plastic wrap. Peel off top sheet; cut pastry into about 15 rounds and fit into greased tart pans. Refrigerate 15 to 20 minutes. Preheat oven to 400 F (200C). Prick pastry shells all over and bake 10 to 15 minutes, until golden. Cool on racks, then remove from pans.

Rinse artichoke hearts well in cold water. Drain, pat dry. Cut in quarters. Cut beef slices in strips and roll each into a cylinder. Stir together sour cream and dill. To assemble, spoon a little of the mixture into each shell. Top with artichokes and beef. Cut each red pepper strip in half crosswise and add to the tarts.

Makes about 15.

CHICKEN SATAY

1 lb. skinned, boned chicken breasts
1/2 teaspoon sambal oelek (hot-pepper paste)
1 teaspoon grated fresh gingerroot
2 tablespoons lemon juice
3 tablespoons dark soy sauce
2 tablespoons honey
1 tablespoon peanut butter
1/2 cup water
Cherries and Italian parsley, if desired

Cut chicken in 1-inch chunks and thread chunks equally on 15 bamboo skewers. Set aside.

In a large saucepan or skillet combine sambal oelek, gingerroot, lemon juice, soy sauce, honey, peanut butter and water. Bring to a boil, stirring constantly, then reduce heat and add as many chicken skewers as will fit without crowding. Simmer 10 minutes, basting. Remove from pan and transfer to a rimmed platter. Repeat with remaining chicken skewers.

Simmer sauce remaining in pan until reduced to about 3/4 cup. Pour over chicken. Cover and refrigerate until cold, then serve. If desired garnish with cherries and Italian parsley.

Makes 15.

— SAGE & ONION PINWHEELS —

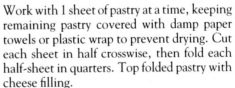

1 (8-oz.) pkg. cream cheese, room temperature
30 fresh, tender sage leaves
3 tablespoons chopped green onions
Freshly ground pepper to taste
Crackers or melba toast, if desired.

On a sheet of aluminum foil spread out cream cheese to an 8-inch square.

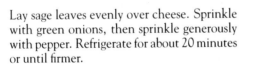

Lay sage leaves evenly over cheese. Sprinkle with green onions, then sprinkle generously with pepper. Refrigerate for about 20 minutes or until firmer.

Using foil as a guide, roll up cheese, jelly-roll style, making a compact log. Refrigerate until firm. To serve, cut crosswise in about 3/8-inch-thick slices. Serve plain or on crackers or melba toast.

Makes about 20.

Variation: If tender sage leaves are unavailable, substitute chopped parsley, tender basil leaves or any other suitable herb.

— CHEESE FILO PASTRIES —

1 lb. feta cheese
3 tablespoons chopped parsley
Freshly ground pepper to taste
3 eggs, beaten
1/2 cup butter, melted
8 sheets filo pastry

Crumble cheese into a bowl. Add parsley, pepper and eggs. Mix well. Brush two 10" x 15" rimmed baking sheets with melted butter. Preheat oven to 400F (200C).

Work with 1 sheet of pastry at a time, keeping remaining pastry covered with damp paper towels or plastic wrap to prevent drying. Cut each sheet in half crosswise, then fold each half-sheet in quarters. Top folded pastry with cheese filling.

Shape pastry around filling like a money bag to enclose. Arrange pastries on buttered baking sheets and brush tops with remaining butter. Bake 20 to 25 minutes or until golden. Serve hot.

Makes 16.

EGGS WITH ANCHOVY DRESSING

FRITTATA

3 ounces arugula or other lettuce leaves
4 hard-cooked eggs, halved
1 teaspoon finely chopped Italian parsley
1 teaspoon snipped fresh chives
ANCHOVY DRESSING:
5 anchovy fillets canned in oil, drained
1/3 cup mayonnaise
3 to 4 tablespoons milk
Freshly ground pepper

1 large russet potato, about 10 ounces
2 tablespoons butter
2 tablespoons vegetable oil
1 small onion, chopped
1 red bell pepper, diced
3 tablespoons chopped fresh herbs such as basil,
    oregano, mint, parsley, sage or thyme
4 eggs, beaten
Salt and freshly ground pepper
Fresh herb sprigs and lettuce leaves to garnish

Cut potatoes into 1-inch pieces. Boil in salted water 12 to 15 minutes until tender. Drain thoroughly, then mash; set aside.

To make dressing, put anchovy fillets in a small bowl. Mash with a fork, then blend in mayonnaise, adding milk to give a creamy consistency. Season with freshly ground pepper.

Heat half of the butter and half of the oil in a large skillet over low heat. Add onion and bell pepper and cook 5 minutes to soften, but do not brown. Add to mashed potatoes with herbs and eggs. Season with salt and freshly ground pepper.

Arrange lettuce leaves and egg halves on a serving plate. Spoon dressing over and around eggs and sprinkle with herbs.

Makes 4 servings.

Preheat broiler. Heat remaining butter and oil in a large nonstick skillet. Add potato mixture, spreading it evenly with a spatula. Cook over medium heat about 4 minutes until the bottom is set and lightly browned. Put under the hot broiler until the top of the frittata is set and golden. Serve hot or cold cut into wedges and garnished with fresh herb sprigs and lettuce leaves.

Makes 4 to 6 servings.

PEPPERED PECORINO CHEESE

1 pound pecorino cheese
3 tablespoons peppercorns, lightly crushed
1 teaspoon finely grated lemon peel (optional)
2/3 cup extra-virgin olive oil
Italian parsley sprig to garnish

Remove rind from cheese and discard. Cut cheese into 1-inch cubes. Put into a shallow dish.

Sprinkle peppercorns and lemon peel, if using, over cheese. Add oil.

Cover dish with foil and refrigerate 2 hours, basting cheese occasionally. Remove from refrigerator 30 minutes before serving. Garnish with parsley sprig.

Makes 6 to 8 servings.

Note: This dish can be kept covered in the refrigerator up to 4 days, but it is important to return it to room temperature 30 minutes before serving.

MOZZARELLA FRITTERS

1 pound mozzarella cheese
3/4 cup all-purpose flour
1 teaspoon paprika
Salt and freshly ground pepper
2 eggs, beaten
2 cups dried bread crumbs
Peanut oil or vegetable oil for deep-frying
Sage leaves to garnish

Cut mozzarella cheese into 1-1/2-inch cubes. Mix flour, paprika, salt and freshly ground pepper in a shallow dish. Put eggs into a second shallow dish and bread crumbs into a third dish.

Coat cheese cubes lightly in the seasoned flour. Dip into eggs, then into bread crumbs to coat evenly. Repeat once more with eggs and bread crumbs.

Half-fill a deep-fat fryer with oil. Preheat to 350F (175C). Deep-fry a few cheese cubes at a time about 2 minutes until golden. Using a slotted spoon, transfer to paper towels to drain. Serve hot garnished with sage leaves.

Makes 4 to 6 servings.

EGG & WALNUT SALAD

ITALIAN CHEESE DIP

1 head leaf lettuce
6 tomatoes, coarsely chopped
1/2 red onion, thinly sliced
16 pitted ripe olives, halved
1/3 cup walnut pieces
4 hard-cooked eggs, quartered
1 tablespoon chopped fennel tops
1 tablespoon snipped fresh chives
DRESSING:
3 tablespoons extra-virgin olive oil
2 tablespoons walnut oil
2 tablespoons red wine vinegar
1 teaspoon whole-grain mustard
Pinch of sugar
Salt and freshly ground pepper

1/2 red bell pepper
1/2 yellow bell pepper
2 ounces dolcelatte cheese
2 ounces mascarpone cheese
1 tablespoon lemon juice
2 small dill pickles, finely chopped
Salt and freshly ground pepper
Breadsticks and a selection of cooked and raw
    vegetables to serve

Tear lettuce into bite-size pieces and put in a salad bowl with tomatoes, onion, olives, walnuts, eggs and herbs. Toss gently to mix.

Preheat broiler. Cook bell peppers skin-side up under the hot broiler 5 to 7 minutes, until skins are evenly blistered and charred. Transfer to a plastic bag a few minutes and then peel away and discard skins. Finely chop flesh and set aside.

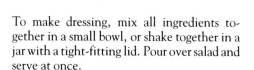

To make dressing, mix all ingredients together in a small bowl, or shake together in a jar with a tight-fitting lid. Pour over salad and serve at once.

Makes 4 to 6 servings.

Put dolcelatte cheese in a small bowl and mash with a fork. Mix in mascarpone cheese and lemon juice until blended, then fold in the chopped bell peppers and dill pickles. Season with salt and freshly ground pepper. Serve with Breadsticks and a selection of cooked and raw vegetables.

Makes 4 servings.

—POACHED EGGS FLORENTINE—

—BAKED EGGS WITH RICOTTA—

4 eggs
2 tablespoons white wine vinegar
2 tablespoons butter
12 ounces spinach leaves, rinsed and finely shredded
1/3 cup whipping cream
2 tablespoons Dijon-style mustard
2 teaspoons chopped Italian parsley
Salt and freshly ground pepper
Hot buttered toast to serve
Paprika and Italian parsley sprigs to garnish

2 tablespoons butter, melted
1/2 cup ricotta cheese
2 teaspoons snipped fresh chives
4 eggs
1/4 cup whipping cream
Salt and freshly ground pepper
Whole chives to garnish

Preheat oven to 350F (175C). Use butter to grease 4 small individual heatproof dishes. Divide ricotta cheese among dishes, levelling surface with a teaspoon. Sprinkle cheese with chives.

Preheat the oven to 250F (120C). To poach eggs, fill a large saucepan with water to a depth of 2 inches. Add vinegar and bring to a boil. Reduce heat to low. Crack an egg onto a saucer and slide egg into pan. Repeat with another egg. Poach 2 eggs at a time 3 to 4 minutes until cooked as desired. Using a slotted spoon, transfer to a warmed plate and put on lowest shelf in the warm oven. Cook remaining 2 eggs in same way, add to plate and place in the warm oven.

Break an egg into each dish and top with cream. Season with salt and freshly ground pepper.

Melt butter in a saucepan. Add spinach and cook, stirring, 1 to 2 minutes until just wilted. Drain off any excess liquid, then stir in remaining ingredients except toast and garnish. Serve spinach and poached eggs accompanied by hot buttered toast. Sprinkle eggs with paprika and garnish with Italian parsley sprigs.

Makes 4 servings.

Place dishes in a shallow baking pan half-filled with warm water. Bake in preheated oven 10 to 12 minutes until eggs are cooked as desired. Garnish with whole chives.

Makes 4 servings.

FONDUTA

STUFFED EGGS

1 pound fontina cheese, diced
1-1/4 cups milk
1/4 cup unsalted butter, melted
4 large egg yolks
Freshly ground pepper
Breadsticks, crusty bread or toast for dipping
Italian parsley sprig to garnish

Place cheese and milk in a bowl. Refrigerate at least 2 hours to soften. Transfer to a double boiler or heatproof bowl set over a pan of simmering water; heat until cheese melts and becomes stringy. Stir in butter and remove from heat.

Beat egg yolks in a small bowl. Stir in a little of the hot cheese mixture, then pour back into the remaining cheese mixture. Return to the heat and beat vigorously until smooth, creamy and thickened. Season with freshly ground pepper.

Transfer to a serving dish (the dish is usually kept hot at table over a candle or small burner), and serve with breadsticks, crusty bread or toast for dipping. Garnish with parsley sprig.

Makes 6 servings.

Note: If fontina cheese is not available a mixture of 8 ounces Gruyere cheese and 8 ounces Edam cheese is a good substitute.

6 eggs
1/3 cup soft cheese with garlic and herbs (3 ounces)
3 tablespoons half and half
1 tablespoon snipped fresh chives
Salt and freshly ground pepper
Sliced ripe olives and chives to garnish
Mixed lettuce leaves to serve

Place eggs in a medium-size saucepan. Cover with water and bring to a boil. Reduce heat and simmer about 10 minutes until hard-cooked.

Drain eggs and place under cold running water until cool. Peel eggs; cut in half lengthwise. Remove yolks from eggs, and put into a small bowl. Mash with a fork.

Add cheese, half and half and chives and mix until smooth. Season with salt and freshly ground pepper. Spoon or pipe into egg whites and garnish with ripe olives and chives. Serve with lettuce leaves.

Makes 4 to 6 servings.

MOZZARELLA SALAD

1 pound mozzarella cheese
2 red onions, thinly sliced
1 tablespoon chopped Italian parsley
1 tablespoon chopped basil or 1 teaspoon dried leaf basil
1 tablespoon snipped fresh chives
1 teaspoon chopped mint
1 (1-3/4-oz.) can anchovy fillets in oil, drained
Italian parsley sprig to garnish
DRESSING:
5 tablespoons extra-virgin olive oil
1 tablespoon white wine vinegar
1 teaspoon balsamic vinegar
1/2 garlic clove, crushed
Salt and freshly ground pepper

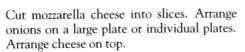

Cut mozzarella cheese into slices. Arrange onions on a large plate or individual plates. Arrange cheese on top.

Sprinkle chopped herbs over cheese. To make dressing, mix all ingredients together in a small bowl, or shake in a jar with a tight-fitting lid. Pour over salad. Arrange anchovy fillets on cheese and herbs in a lattice pattern and serve at once garnished with parsley sprig.

Makes 4 to 6 servings.

EGG & OLIVE SALAD

1 pound small new potatoes
3 hard-cooked eggs, halved or quartered
1/2 head romaine lettuce
18 pitted ripe olives, halved
Salt and freshly ground pepper
1/3 cup mayonnaise
1 (1-3/4-oz.) can anchovy fillets in oil, drained
Paprika to garnish

Cook potatoes in boiling, salted water 12 to 15 minutes until tender. Drain and cool completely.

Halve or quarter potatoes and arrange with eggs, lettuce and olives on a serving plate or individual plates. Season with salt and freshly ground pepper.

Spoon mayonnaise over salad and arrange anchovy fillets on top. Sprinkle with a little paprika. Refrigerate 1 hour before serving.

Makes 6 servings.

MARINATED SOFT CHEESE

RICOTTA MOLDS

3/4 cup ricotta cheese (6 ounces)
6 ounces cream cheese, softened
8 Italian parsley sprigs, coarsely chopped
8 basil sprigs
1 tablespoon chopped oregano or 1 teaspoon dried leaf oregano
2 garlic cloves, chopped
1/4 teaspoon hot pepper flakes
Juice of 1/2 lemon
10 peppercorns, lightly crushed
2/3 cup extra-virgin olive oil
Fresh grape leaves to serve (optional)
Oregano sprigs to garnish

1-1/2 cups ricotta cheese (12 ounces)
1 tablespoon finely chopped Italian parsley
1 tablespoon chopped fennel tops
1 tablespoon snipped fresh chives
1 tablespoon unflavored gelatin powder
3 tablespoons water
2/3 cup mayonnaise
Salt and freshly ground pepper
Fresh herb sprigs to garnish
BELL PEPPER SAUCE:
2 large red bell peppers, broiled, peeled and chopped, page 14
3 tablespoons extra-virgin olive oil
Few drops of balsamic vinegar
Salt and freshly ground pepper

In a small bowl, beat cheeses together with a wooden spoon. Divide into 6 portions and shape into balls or round cakes. Arrange in 1 layer in an oiled shallow dish. Using a blender or food processor, process remaining ingredients, except grape leaves, until fairly smooth.

In a bowl, mix together cheese and herbs. Oil 6 (about 1/2-cup) molds. In a small bowl, soften gelatin in water 5 minutes. Place bowl over a saucepan of simmering water and stir until dissolved. Cool slightly, then stir into cheese mixture with mayonnaise, salt and freshly ground pepper. Divide among oiled molds, cover and refrigerate until set.

Pour over cheeses. Cover dish with foil and refrigerate 3 hours, basting cheeses occasionally. Remove from refrigerator 30 minutes before serving on a bed of grape leaves, if using. Garnish with oregano sprigs.

Makes 6 servings.

Note: If available, 1-1/2 cups Italian straccino or robiola can replace the cheeses in the recipe.

To make sauce, put bell peppers and oil in a food processor or blender and process until smooth. Add balsamic vinegar to taste, and season with salt and freshly ground pepper. Pour into a small bowl, and refrigerate until required. Turn out ricotta molds onto individual plates and serve with sauce. Garnish with herb sprigs.

Makes 6 servings.

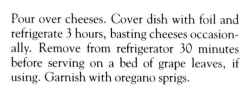

STUFFED CHILES

12 fresh red or green chiles
3 tablespoons extra-virgin olive oil
1 tablespoon white wine vinegar
Mint leaves to garnish
FILLING:
4 sun-dried tomatoes in oil, drained and finely chopped
5 ounces mild soft goat cheese
2 green onions, white part only, finely chopped
2 teaspoons finely chopped mint
1 teaspoon finely chopped basil or 1/3 teaspoon dried
   leaf basil
Salt and freshly ground pepper
Mint leaves to garnish

Preheat broiler. Cook chiles under hot broiler 8 to 10 minutes, turning occasionally, until skins are evenly blistered and charred. Transfer to a plastic bag a few minutes, then peel away and discard skins. Make a lengthwise cut down length of each chile. Carefully rinse out seeds under cold running water. Pat the chiles dry with paper towels.

To make filling, mix ingredients together in a small bowl. Divide filling among chiles and arrange on a serving plate. Drizzle with olive oil and vinegar. Cover and refrigerate at least 30 minutes. Garnish with mint leaves.

Makes 4 to 6 servings.

FAVA BEANS WITH GOAT CHEESE

1/4 cup extra-virgin olive oil
1 onion, chopped
2 pounds fresh fava beans, shelled, or 12 ounces frozen
   fava beans, thawed
1 tablespoon chopped rosemary
Salt and freshly ground pepper
2 heads Belgian endive or 1 head radicchio
1 (8-oz.) goat cheese log, sliced
Rosemary sprigs to garnish

Heat oil in a large skillet, add onion and cook over medium heat about 10 minutes until soft and golden. Stir in beans and rosemary.

Add enough water to just cover beans and season with salt and freshly ground pepper. Bring to a boil, reduce heat, cover and simmer 12 to 15 minutes, stirring frequently, until beans are very tender and liquid is absorbed.

Preheat broiler. Slice endive or radicchio and stir into hot beans. Lay cheese slices on top of bean mixture. Put skillet under hot broiler 2 to 3 minutes until cheese is browned. Serve hot garnished with rosemary sprigs.

Makes 4 to 6 servings.

CHEESE STRAWS

6 tablespoons butter, room temperature
3/4 cup shredded Cheddar cheese (3 oz.)
1 cup all-purpose flour
1 teaspoon paprika
Red (cayenne) pepper to taste

In a medium bowl, cream butter until fluffy; beat in cheese. Blend in flour. Divide dough in thirds; wrap each portion in plastic wrap and refrigerate until firm enough to roll.

Preheat oven to 350F (180C). Roll out 1 portion of dough at a time, keeping remaining dough refrigerated. To roll out each portion of dough, dust 2 sheets of plastic wrap with flour; roll out dough between floured sheets of plastic wrap to about 1/8 inch thick. Peel off top sheet of plastic. Cut rolled-out dough in 4-inch long, 1/2-inch-wide strips. Hold each strip at both ends; twist in opposite directions so each strip has 2 twists. Arrange twists on ungreased baking trays.

Mix paprika and red pepper. Using a dry pastry brush, dab paprika mixture onto cheese straws. Bake 10 minutes or until golden brown around edges.

Makes about 80.

Tip: Very short doughs like this one are much easier to roll out if you roll them between sheets of plastic wrap. (This is especialy true in hot weather.)

MUSHROOMS & BLUE CHEESE

12 to 14 small fresh mushrooms
4 oz. blue-veined cheese
4 oz. cream cheese, room temperature
1 tablespoon half and half
Pecan halves and parsley sprigs or basil leaves

Cut stems out of mushrooms, then wipe mushrooms with a cloth dipped in cold acidulated water (1-1/2 teaspoons lemon juice or distilled white vinegar to 2 cups water). Reserve stems for other uses, if desired. Set mushrooms aside.

Crumble blue-veined cheese into a medium bowl. Add cream cheese; beat until mixture is smooth, then add half and half and beat until fluffy. Spoon into a pastry bag fitted with a star tip, If preparing ahead, refrigerate cheese mixture in pastry bag; also cover and refrigerate mushrooms.

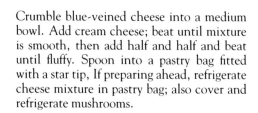

To serve, arrange mushrooms, capside down, on a serving plate. Pipe cheese mixture into hollow of each mushroom; top each with a pecan half and a parsley sprig or a basil leaf.

Makes 12 to 14.

—CHEESE & ONION PASTRIES—

**1-1/2 cups (all-purpose) flour
1/2 teaspoon salt
1/2 cup cold water
2 tablespoons butter
1 cup chopped green onions including tops
About 1/8 teaspoon red (cayenne) pepper
4 oz. Gouda cheese
1 egg, beaten
Vegetable oil for deep-frying**

In a bowl, stir together flour and salt. Then stir in cold water to make a firm dough. Turn out onto a lightly floured surface, knead until smooth. Wrap in plastic wrap; let rest 30 minutes.

Melt butter in a skillet; add green onions. Cook, stirring, until soft. Remove from heat and stir in red pepper. Set aside. Cut cheese in 24 equal cubes. Divide dough into 24 equal portions. On a lightly floured board, roll out each portion into a 4-inch round.

Spoon green-onion mixture evenly onto dough rounds, then top each round with a cheese cube. Brush edges of each round with egg; fold in half over filling and press edges with a fork to seal. In a deep, heavy saucepan, heat about 2 inches of oil to 350F (180C) or until a 1-inch bread cube turns golden brown in about 65 seconds. Add pastries, a few at a time, and cook until golden on all sides. Drain on paper towels and serve warm.

Makes 24.

—CHEESE BITES—

**8 oz. Cheddar cheese
6 to 10 bacon slices
40 fresh sage or basil leaves**

Cut cheese in 40 equal cubes. Cut bacon slices in pieces long enough to wrap around cheese cubes.

Wrap 1 sage or basil leaf around each cheese cube, then wrap in 1 piece of bacon. Secure with wooden picks. Lightly grease a large skillet; add as many bacon rolls as will fit without crowding. Cook over medium heat until bacon is crisp, Drain on paper towels. Repeat with remaining bacon rolls. Serve hot or warm; provide small napkins.

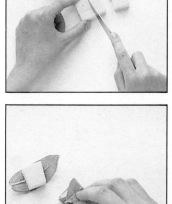

Makes 40.

CHEESE AND PEPPERONI BITES
In place of sage or basil leaves, use small, thin pepperoni slices.

PEPPER-CHEESE ROUNDS

SESAME CHEESE BALLS

8 oz. Cheddar cheese
1 (8-oz.) pkg. cream cheese, room temperature
1/4 cup dry sherry
6 tablespoons coarsely cracked pepper
Toast rounds and cooked, shelled, deveined shrimp
Tomato wedges

Finely shred Cheddar cheese into a large bowl; beat Cheddar cheese and cream cheese until smooth and well blended. Gradually beat in sherry. Cover and refrigerate until firm.

About 1/2 cup slivered almonds or pepitas
7 tablespoons sesame seeds
1 (8-oz.) pkg. cream cheese, room temperature
2 tablespoons grated Parmesan cheese
2 teaspoons instant minced onion
Salt and freshly ground pepper to taste
Tomato wedges and Italian parsley

Preheat oven to 350F (180C). Spread almonds on a baking sheet; bake about 10 minutes or until golden. Cool. Place sesame seeds in a dry skillet and stir over medium heat until golden. Remove from heat; cool.

Divide chilled cheese mixture into 4 equal portions. Place each on a sheet of plastic wrap or wax paper and shape into a 2-inch log. (Or shape cheese into balls.)

In a bowl, beat together cream cheese, Parmesan cheese and onion. Season with salt and pepper. Cover with plastic wrap and refrigerate 20 minutes or until firm. Stir in cooled sesame seeds, then shape mixture into 25 equal balls.

Spread pepper on a sheet of plastic wrap or wax paper. Roll cheese logs in pepper to coat all sides, gently pressing pepper into cheese. Wrap individually and refrigerate until ready to serve. To serve, cut logs in about 3/8-inch-thick slices. Place each slice on a toast round and top with a shrimp. Or serve slices plain and garnish with tomato wedges.

Makes about 20 slices.

Spread toasted almonds on a sheet of wax paper; roll cheese balls in nuts to coat. Arrange on a plate, cover and refrigerate (or keep in a cool place) until ready to serve. Garnish with tomato wedges and Italian parsley.

Makes 25.

APRICOT-NUT CHEESE

1 (8-oz.) pkg. cream cheese, room temperature
1/2 cup moist-pack dried apricots, cut in small pieces
6 tablespoons whole hazelnuts
1/4 cup poppy seeds or toasted sesame seeds
Crackers or apple wedges, if desired
Italian parsley

In a bowl, beat cream cheese until smooth. Add apricots and beat to blend well. Preheat oven to 350F (180C). Spread hazelnuts evenly on a rimmed baking sheet and bake about 10 minutes or until lightly toasted. Cool.

Pour nuts onto a paper towel, fold towel around nuts and rub briskly between your palms to remove as much of skins as possible (it's impossible to get them all off). Return nuts to oven and bake 5 minutes longer or until golden. Cool, chop coarsely and add to cheese.

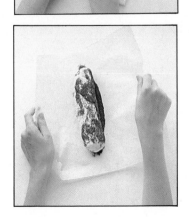

On a sheet of plastic wrap or wax paper, form cheese mixture into an 8-inch-long log. Sprinkle poppy seeds or toasted sesame seeds over cheese log, then roll log so all sides are coated with seeds. Wrap log and refrigerate until firm. To serve, place log on a cheese board and cut in about 3/8-inch-thick slices. Garnish with Italian parsley.

Makes about 20 slices.

BASIL-CHEESE TOASTS

2 tomatoes
1 (2-oz.) can flat anchovy fillets
10 slices French bread
1 cup shredded Gruyère cheese (4 oz.)
Freshly ground pepper to taste
1/4 cup shredded fresh basil leaves
1/4 cup olive oil
Basil sprigs

Thinly slice tomatoes. If tomatoes are large, cut each slice in half. Drain anchovies and cut in strips. Set tomatoes and anchovies aside.

Lightly oil a large, shallow baking dish. Preheat oven to 400F (200C). Arrange bread slices in oiled baking dish; sprinkle evenly with cheese. Arrange anchovy strips over cheese; top each bread slice with 1 or 2 tomato slices.

Sprinkle with pepper and some of basil. Drizzle oil over all. Bake 10 to 15 minutes or until bread is crisp and cheese is melted. Sprinkle with remaining basil and garnish with basil sprigs. Serve hot.

Makes 10.

EGG & CHIVE PINWHEELS

EGGS TAPENADE

1 (about 1-lb.) loaf unsliced white bread
1/2 cup butter, room temperature
6 hard-cooked eggs
3 tablespoons mayonnaise
1 teaspoon prepared hot mustard
Salt and pepper to taste
6 tablespoons chopped chives
Italian parsley

6 hard-cooked eggs
18 ripe olives
5 flat anchovy fillets
1 tablespoon drained capers
1 (3-1/4-oz.) can tuna, drained
3 tablespoons olive oil
Lemon juice to taste
12 Italian parsley leaves

Using an electric or serrated knife, trim top of loaf to make it flat. Cut off all crusts, then cut loaf lengthwise in 5 equal slices. Reserve bread trimmings for bread crumbs or other uses, if desired. Spread 1 side of each slice with butter. Set aside.

Shell eggs and cut each in half cross-wise, using a silver or stainless steel knife (carbon steel leaves black marks on egg white). Remove yolks and place in a food processor fitted with a metal blade. Trim bases of whites so eggs will sit flat. Set whites aside.

Shell eggs, cut in chunks and place in a bowl. Add mayonnaise and mustard. Mash ingredients together thoroughly; season with salt and pepper. Spread egg mixture evenly over buttered side of each bread slice, spreading almost to edges. Sprinkle with chives.

Remove pits from 12 olives, then place olives, anchovies, capers and drained tuna in food processor with egg yolks. Process until well blended. With motor running, gradually add oil to make a thick puree. Season with lemon juice. If preparing ahead, cover yolk mixture and refrigerate up to 2 days; place egg whites in a bowl, add cold water to cover and refrigerate up to 2 days. Drain whites, pat dry and fill just before serving.

Roll up each slice jelly-roll style, starting with short side. Wrap each roll in plastic wrap and refrigerate until ready to serve. To serve, using a serrated or electric knife, cut each roll crosswise in 5 or 6 lengths. Arrange on a platter and garnish with parsley.

To fill whites, spoon egg-yolk mixture into cavity of each one. Cut remaining 6 olives in half; place 1 half atop each filled egg half. Garnish with an Italian parsley leaf.

Makes 25 to 30.

Makes 12.

DEVILED EGGS

12 eggs
1 teaspoon prepared hot mustard
6 tablespoons mayonnaise
Few drops of hot-pepper sauce
Pinch of red (cayenne) pepper
2 teaspoons paprika
Rolled anchovy fillets or chopped parsley or other herb,
    to garnish

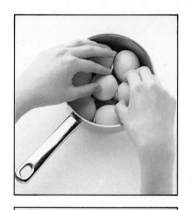

To boil eggs so yolks are centered, tightly pack them into a saucepan, pointed end down. (You may need to cook eggs in 2 batches.) Pour in enough cold water to cover. Bring to a boil; reduce heat, cover and simmer 10 minutes.

Drain eggs and rinse under cold running water until cool enough to handle. (Quick cooling prevents a black ring forming around yolk.) Shell eggs, then cut each in half lengthwise with a stainless steel or silver knife (carbon steel leaves black marks on egg whites). Place yolks in a bowl and add mustard, mayonnaise, hot-pepper sauce, red pepper and paprika. Mash ingredients together to blend well. Season. Spoon mixture into pastry bag with a fluted tip.

If preparing ahead, refrigerate mixture in pastry bag; place egg whites in a bowl, add cold water to cover and refrigerate. Drain whites, pat dry and fill yolk mixture into cavity of each one; garnish.

Makes 24.

EGG & SESAME ROLLS

3 eggs
1/4 teaspoon salt
1 tablespoon water
2 tablespoons sesame seeds
2 teaspoons dark soy sauce
1/4 teaspoon sugar
Salt to taste
1/2 small onion, finely chopped
1 tablespoon vegetable oil
1 (8-oz.) package frozen chopped spinach, thawed
1 thick slice cooked ham, cut in thirds

Lightly beat egg with salt and water; make 3 thin omelets in a 6-inch skillet. Stir sesame seeds in a dry pan over low heat until golden, then grind while hot. Add soy and sugar. Gently cook onion in a little oil. Add drained spinach and season to taste. Cool.

Place 1 omelet on rounded side of bamboo placemat. Spread 1/3 of the spinach mixture on 1 end; do not spread to edge. Sprinkle with 1/3 of the sesame seed mixture; place ham strip down center.

Use placemat to help roll omelet; set aside to rest for several minutes wrapped in placemat. Unroll the placemat. Repeat with remaining 2 omelets. Using a sharp knife carefully slice each omelet in four 1-1/4-inch wide slices.

Makes 12.

AIOLI & CRUDITÉS

4 garlic cloves
About 1/2 teaspoon salt
2 egg yolks
1 cup olive oil
Juice of 1/2 lemon
Crisp raw vegetables, such as carrot sticks, celery
   sticks, small whole radishes, cauliflowerets, edible-
   pod peas, cucumber sticks, blanched fresh asparagus
   spears and green onions.

Press garlic through a garlic press into a bowl. Add 1/2 teaspoon salt and egg yolks; beat well with a whisk. Add 1 or 2 drops oil and whisk well.

Gradually add about 2 more tablespoons oil, whisking constantly. Then, still whisking constantly, add remaining oil in a thin stream. If mixture becomes too thick, add a little hot water. When all oil has been added, whisk in lemon juice and season with additional salt, if needed. Cover aioli and refrigerate until ready to use.

Prepare the uncooked vegetables; cut the carrots in 3-inch sticks, slice the cucumber and trim the celery, radishes, cauliflowers and green onions. To serve, spoon aioli into a serving bowl and place in center of a large platter. Arrange vegetables around aioli; dip vegetables in aioli before eating.

Makes about 1 cup aioli.

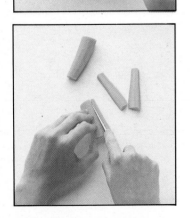

EGG & CAVIAR SPREAD

4 eggs
1/4 cup butter
Salt and freshly ground pepper to taste
1/2 cup dairy sour cream
4 green onions or 1/2 small white onion, finely chopped
3 tablespoons black caviar
Crackers

Place eggs in a saucepan and pour in enough cold water to cover. Bring to a boil; then reduce heat, cover and simmer 10 minutes. Drain eggs and rinse under cold running water until cool enough to handle. Shell eggs, cut in chunks and place in a bowl.

Melt butter in a small saucepan. Mash eggs thoroughly; pour hot melted butter over warm mashed eggs. Season with salt and pepper. Pack egg mixture into a serving dish; cover and refrigerate up to 24 hours.

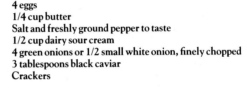

Just before serving, in a small bowl, stir together sour cream and green onion or white onion. Spread over egg mixture. Top with caviar. If desired, garnish with lemon or lime slices or wedges and parsley sprigs. Serve with crackers; provide a small knife for spreading.

Makes 1-1/2 to 2 cups.

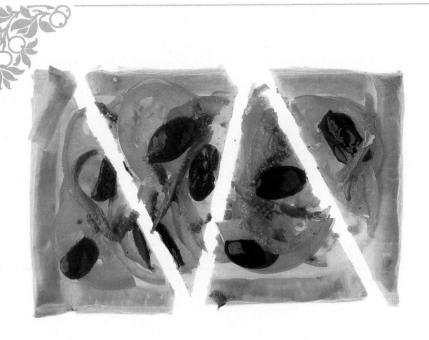

PISSALADIÈRE

MINI-PIZZAS

3 sheets (1-1/2 x 17-1/2 oz. pkg.) frozen puff pastry, thawed
3 or 4 tomatoes
Freshly ground pepper to taste
6 to 8 calamatta olives
1 (2 oz.) can flat anchovy fillets, drained
1 egg, beaten
Chopped fresh basil, if desired

Unfold pastry sheets. Cut each sheet of pastry into two 5" x 6" rectangles. Arrange rectangles on ungreased baking sheets. Cut pastry trimmings in 1/2-inch wide strips and place along edges of pastry rectangles to form borders.

Prick centers of pastry rectangles with a fork.

1 (1/4-oz.) pkg. active dry yeast
1 teaspoon sugar
1 cup warm water (110F, 45C)
2-1/2 cups all-purpose flour
1/2 teaspoon salt
2 tablespoons vegetable oil
2 onions, chopped
2 garlic cloves, crushed
4 to 6 tomatoes, peeled, sliced
2 teaspoons tomato paste
Salt and pepper to taste
1/4 lb. sliced pepperoni, cut in small pieces
4 oz. mozzarella cheese, cut in cubes
20 pitted ripe olives

Dissolve yeast and sugar with 1/2 cup warm water. Let stand until bubbly. Stir together flour and 1/2 teaspoon salt. Mix in yeast mixture and remaining 1/2 cup warm water. Knead on a well-floured board at least 5 minutes or until smooth and elastic. Place dough in greased bowl and turn.

Cover and let rise in a warm place about 1 hour or until doubled in bulk. Heat oil in a large skillet. Add onions and garlic; cook, stirring, 2 minutes. Stir in tomatoes and simmer, uncovered, 20 minutes. Add tomato paste and season.

Preheat oven to 400F (200C). Halve tomatoes, then thinly slice crosswise. Arrange tomatoes in even rows on pastries, slightly overlapping slices. Sprinkle generously with pepper. Cut olive flesh away from pits; arrange olives and anchovies over tomatoes. Brush borders of pastries with egg. Bake 10-15 minutes or until pastry is golden. Cut each pastry in 4 triangles and sprinkle with basil, if desired. Serve warm.

Makes 24 pieces.

Preheat oven to 400F (200C). Punch down dough, turn out onto a floured board and knead lightly. Roll out to 1/2-inch thick and cut into 3-inch rounds. Arrange on greased baking sheets. Top with tomato sauce, pepperoni, cheese and olives. Bake 20 to 30 minutes.

Makes 12.

BELL PEPPER PIZZETTES

PIZZA DOUGH:
4 cups bread flour or all-purpose flour
Pinch of salt
1 (1/4-oz.) package active dry yeast (about
    1 tablespoon)
1 teaspoon sugar
Scant 1 cup warm water (110F, 45C)
2 tablespoons extra-virgin olive oil
Oregano sprigs to garnish
TOPPING:
2 red or yellow bell peppers
3 tablespoons sun-dried tomato paste
1/4 cup capers in wine vinegar, drained
2 tablespoons chopped fresh oregano or 2 teaspoons
    dried leaf oregano
Salt and freshly ground pepper

Preheat oven to 450F (230C). Oil 2 baking sheets. Turn out dough onto a lightly floured surface. Knead gently and cut into 16 equal pieces. Roll each piece into a small oval about 1/4 inch thick.

Sift flour and salt into a large bowl. In a small bowl, dissolve yeast and sugar in water. Let stand 5 to 10 minutes until frothy. Stir in olive oil. Using a wooden spoon, gradually stir yeast mixture into flour to give a soft, but not sticky, dough. Knead on a floured surface 5 minutes until smooth and elastic. Place in an oiled medium-size bowl, cover and let rise in a warm place 35 to 40 minutes until doubled in size.

Transfer to the baking sheets and prick dough with a fork. Divide sun-dried tomato paste, reserved peppers, capers and oregano among dough ovals. Season with salt and freshly ground pepper. Bake in preheated oven 8 to 10 minutes until golden. Serve hot or warm garnished with oregano sprigs.

Makes 16 pizzettes.

Meanwhile, preheat broiler. Cook bell peppers under hot broiler about 10 minutes, turning occasionally, until skins are evenly blistered and charred. Transfer peppers to a plastic bag a few minutes, then peel away and discard skins. Cut peppers into strips. Set aside.

Red Onion & Gorgonzola Pizzettes In place of above topping, use 1-1/2 cups (4 ounces) crumbled Gorgonzola cheese, 1/2 chopped red onion and 2 tablespoons chopped thyme.

Shrimp & Fennel Pizzettes Replace bell peppers, capers and herbs with 1 small roasted fennel bulb, 4 ounces cooked shrimp and 2 teaspoons fennel seeds. To roast fennel, brush with olive oil and place in a preheated 350F (175C) oven 35 to 40 minutes. Cool and chop.

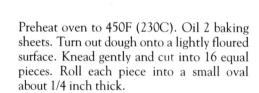

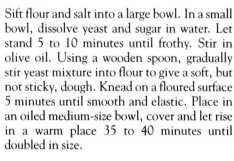

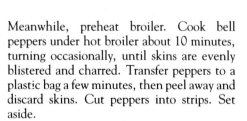

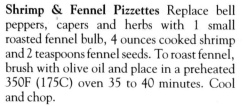

FOCACCIA

BREAD SALAD

4 cups bread flour or all-purpose flour
Pinch of salt
1 (1/4-oz.) package active dry yeast (about 1
   tablespoon)
1 teaspoon sugar
1 cup warm milk (110F, 45C)
1/4 cup extra-virgin olive oil, plus extra for brushing
2 teaspoons rosemary
Coarse sea salt

Sift flour and salt into a large bowl.

8 ounces firm, country-style bread, crusts removed
1 red onion, thinly sliced
1/2 cucumber, peeled and diced
6 small tomatoes, quartered
2 celery stalks, sliced
6 basil sprigs, shredded
9 pitted ripe olives, halved
Salt and freshly ground pepper
5 tablespoons extra-virgin olive oil
2 tablespoons red wine vinegar
1 teaspoon balsamic vinegar

In a small bowl, dissolve yeast and sugar in milk. Let stand 5 to 10 minutes until frothy. Stir in the 1/4 cup olive oil. Using a wooden spoon, gradually beat yeast mixture into flour mixture to give a soft, but not sticky, dough. Knead on a lightly floured surface 5 minutes until smooth and elastic. Place in an oiled medium-size bowl, cover and let rise in a warm place about 40 minutes until doubled in size. Turn out onto a lightly floured surface and knead 5 minutes.

Cut bread into small cubes and place in a large bowl. Sprinkle with enough cold water to moisten thoroughly but do not let bread become soggy.

Oil a baking sheet. Roll out dough to a large circle about 1/2 inch thick and transfer to baking sheet. Brush dough with olive oil, sprinkle with rosemary and sea salt and lightly press into surface. With your finger make deep indentations over surface. Let rise 25 minutes. Preheat oven to 450F (230C). Bake in preheated oven 20 to 25 minutes until golden. Brush again with olive oil. Serve warm.

Makes 1 loaf.

Add onion, cucumber, tomatoes, celery, shredded basil and olives to bowl. Season with salt and freshly ground pepper. In a small bowl, mix together oil and vinegars, then pour over salad. Toss well to mix. Let stand 30 minutes before serving.

Makes 6 servings.

— TOMATO & ONION BREAD —

4 cups bread flour or all-purpose flour
Pinch of salt
1 (1/4-oz.) package active dry yeast (about
   1 tablespoon)
1 teaspoon sugar
Scant 1 cup warm water (110F, 45C)
4 tablespoons extra-virgin olive oil
1 onion, finely chopped
1 garlic clove, crushed
4 ounces sun-dried tomatoes preserved in oil, drained
9 large basil leaves
Freshly ground pepper
Milk to glaze
1 teaspoon coarse sea salt
Basil leaves to garnish

Oil a baking sheet, Heat remaining 1 tablespoon oil in a skillet, add onion and garlic, and cook 3 minutes until softened. Remove skillet from heat and set aside. Turn out dough onto a lightly floured surface and cut in half. Roll out to give 2 rectangles each about 12″ × 9″. Transfer 1 piece to the baking sheet and prick surface with a fork.

Sift flour and salt into a large bowl. In a small bowl, dissolve yeast and sugar in warm water. Let stand 5 to 10 minutes until frothy.

Spread cooked onion mixture over pricked dough, leaving a 1/2-inch border around the edge. Arrange sun-dried tomatoes and basil leaves over onion and season with freshly ground pepper. Moisten edges of dough with a little cold water and cover with second sheet of dough.

Stir 3 tablespoons of the olive oil into yeast mixture. Using a wooden spoon, gradually stir yeast mixture into flour to give a soft, but not sticky, dough. Knead on a lightly floured surface 5 minutes until smooth and elastic. Put dough into an oiled medium-size bowl, cover and let rise in a warm place 35 to 40 minutes until doubled in size.

Crimp dough edges to seal. Using a sharp knife mark a lattice pattern on surface of dough. Brush with a little milk to glaze and sprinkle with coarse sea salt. Let rise 20 minutes. Preheat oven to 450F (230C). Bake loaf in preheated oven about 25 minutes until golden-brown and underside is firm and lightly colored. Serve warm or cold, on its own as part of the antipasti. Cut into pieces and garnish with basil leaves.

Makes 1 large loaf.

GOAT CHEESE TARTS

1 to 2 teaspoons extra-virgin olive oil
2 tablespoons butter
2 cups fresh bread crumbs
1 tablespoon sesame seeds
6 ounces goat cheese
4 sun-dried tomatoes preserved in oil, drained
Salt and freshly ground pepper
4 basil leaves
1 teaspoon finely chopped mint
Mixed lettuce leaves and chives to garnish

Preheat oven to 400F (205C). Use olive oil to grease 4 (3- to 4-inch) tart pans.

Melt butter in a small saucepan, and stir in bread crumbs and sesame seeds. Divide among prepared tart pans, pressing firmly onto bottoms and sides. Bake in preheated oven 12 to 15 minutes until crisp and light golden. Carefully remove tart shells from pans and place on a baking sheet.

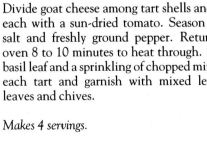

Divide goat cheese among tart shells and top each with a sun-dried tomato. Season with salt and freshly ground pepper. Return to oven 8 to 10 minutes to heat through. Put a basil leaf and a sprinkling of chopped mint on each tart and garnish with mixed lettuce leaves and chives.

Makes 4 servings.

BRUSCHETTA AL POMODORO

8 small thick slices rustic bread
1/4 cup extra-virgin olive oil
1 garlic clove, crushed
2 large tomatoes, chopped
2 tablespoons chopped basil or 2 teaspoons dried leaf basil
Salt and freshly ground pepper
8 anchovy fillets canned in oil, drained (optional)

Preheat oven to 400F (205C). Put bread in 1 layer on a baking sheet. Bake in preheated oven 10 minutes until golden.

Meanwhile warm oil and garlic in a small saucepan.

Drizzle oil and garlic over bread. Divide tomatoes and basil among slices, season with salt and freshly ground pepper and top with anchovy fillets, if using. Serve at once.

Makes 4 servings.

OLIVE BREAD

1 (1/4-oz.) package active dried yeast (about
   1 tablespoon)
1 teaspoon sugar
1-1/3 cups warm water (110F, 45C)
6 cups bread flour or all-purpose flour
Pinch of salt
1 tablespoon chopped oregano or 1 teaspoon dried leaf
   oregano
1/4 cup extra-virgin olive oil, plus extra for brushing
30 pitted green olives

In a small bowl, dissolve yeast and sugar in warm water. Let stand 5 to 10 minutes until frothy.

Sift flour and salt into a large bowl, and stir in oregano. Stir olive oil into yeast mixture. Using a wooden spoon, gradually stir yeast mixture into flour to give a soft, but not sticky, dough. Add a little more warm water if necessary.

Knead dough on a lightly floured surface 5 minutes until elastic. Place in an oiled large bowl, cover and let rise in a warm place about 40 minutes until doubled in size.

Grease 1 large baking sheet, or 2 smaller baking sheets. Turn out dough onto a floured surface. To make 1 large loaf, roll out to a large circle 1 inch thick. Or, cut dough in half and roll out 2 ovals about 1/2 inch thick. Place on the baking sheet or sheets.

With your floured finger, make 30 deep indentations over surface of large loaf, or 15 in each of the smaller ones. Press an olive into each indentation.

Brush with olive oil and let rise 25 minutes. Preheat oven to 450F (230C). Bake loaves in preheated oven 20 to 25 minutes for small loaves, 30 to 35 minutes for large loaf until golden-brown and undersides sound hollow when tapped. Cool on a wire rack. Serve warm or cold as part of the antipasti.

Makes 1 large or 2 small loaves.

CRAB & RICOTTA TARTS

PASTRY DOUGH:
2 cups all-purpose flour
Pinch of salt
1/2 cup butter, chilled, diced
About 1/4 water
FILLING:
8 ounces crabmeat
1 cup ricotta cheese (8 ounces)
3 green onions, finely chopped
2 whole eggs plus 1 yolk
2 tablespoons chopped Italian parsley
Few drops of hot pepper sauce
Salt and freshly ground pepper
Mixed lettuce leaves to serve
Italian parsley sprigs to garnish

Preheat oven to 400F (205C). Sift flour and salt into a small bowl. Rub in butter until mixture resembles bread crumbs. Stir in enough water to make a firm dough. Place dough on a floured surface and knead gently until smooth. Use to line 4 (3- to 4-inch) tart pans. Prick bottoms lightly and chill 20 minutes. Line tart shells with waxed paper and cover with dry beans. Bake in preheated oven 15 minutes, removing beans and paper after 10 minutes.

Remove tart shells from oven and reduce temperature to 350F (175C). To make filling, mix ingredients together in a bowl. Spoon into tart shells. Bake about 20 minutes until set and golden-brown. Serve warm or cold garnished with mixed lettuce leaves and parsley sprigs.

Makes 4 servings.

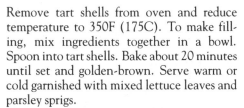

SAVORY PASTRIES

1 recipe Pizza Dough, page 74
Vegetable oil for deep-frying
FILLING:
3 tablespoons sun-dried tomato paste
2 tablespoons olive paste
6 ounces mozzarella cheese, thinly sliced
Freshly ground pepper
1 egg white, lightly beaten
Italian parsley sprigs to garnish

Make dough and let rise until doubled in size. On a lightly floured surface, roll out dough to 1/4 inch thick. Cut out circles using a 4-inch plain round cutter. Spread a little sun-dried tomato paste and Olive Paste onto each round of dough. Cut cheese slices in half and place a piece on each dough circle. Season and freshly ground pepper.

Brush edges of dough circles with a little egg white, then fold dough over filling to make half-moon shapes; press edges together to seal. Half-fill a deep-fat fryer with oil. Preheat to 350F (175C). Deep-fry a few pastries at a time, 2 to 3 minutes, turning once, until golden. Using a slotted spoon, transfer to paper towels to drain. Serve hot garnished with parsley sprigs.

Makes about 12.

WALNUT BREAD

1 (1/4-oz.) package active dry yeast
1 tablespoon honey
2/3 cup warm milk (110F, 45C)
3 cups bread flour or all-purpose flour
3 cups whole-wheat flour
1-1/2 teaspoons salt
2 tablespoons butter, diced
1-1/4 cups chopped walnuts
2 teaspoons fennel seeds, lightly crushed
1/2 teaspoon grated nutmeg
About 1 cup warm water
Milk to glaze

In a small bowl, dissolve yeast and honey in milk. Let stand 5 to 10 minutes until frothy.

Sift flours and salt into a large bowl. Rub butter into flour. Stir in walnuts, 1 teaspoon of the fennel seeds and the grated nutmeg.

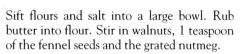

Using a wooden spoon, stir yeast mixture into flour mixture, then gradually beat in enough water to form a soft, but not sticky, dough.

Knead dough on a lightly floured surface 5 minutes until elastic. Put dough into an oiled large bowl, cover and let rise in a warm place 35 to 40 minutes until doubled in size. Turn out onto a lightly floured surface and knead 5 minutes.

Preheat oven to 425F (220C). Oil a 6-inch round pan. Divide dough into 7 equal pieces and shape into balls. Arrange balls in oiled pan. Brush tops with milk and sprinkle with remaining 1 teaspoon fennel seeds. Let rise in a warm place 25 minutes. Bake in preheated oven about 45 minutes until browned and bottom sounds hollow when tapped.

Turn bread out onto a wire rack and cool. Serve as part of the antipasti.

Makes 1 large loaf.

Note: This bread is delicious served with cheese and fish dishes, for soaking up olive oil dressings and is particularly good toasted.

MOZZARELLA TOASTS

12 thick slices French or Italian bread
1/3 cup extra-virgin olive oil
1 teaspoon finely chopped Italian parsley
14 anchovy fillets canned in oil, drained
1 pound mozzarella cheese, cut into 12 slices
Freshly ground pepper
Italian parsley sprigs to garnish

Preheat broiler. Arrange bread in 1 layer on a baking sheet, then toast both sides under preheated broiler until golden.

Meanwhile put oil, parsley and 2 of the anchovy fillets in a small saucepan. Heat gently to warm, stirring with a fork to break up anchovies. Drizzle oil mixture over toasted bread and put a slice of cheese on each one. Season with freshly ground pepper.

Garnish with remaining anchovy fillets and return to broiler 2 to 3 minutes until cheese is hot and bubbling. Serve at once garnished with Italian parsley sprigs.

Makes 6 servings.

OLIVE PASTE TOASTS

4 large thick slices rustic bread
3 tablespoons extra-virgin olive oil
1/2 garlic clove, crushed
Red bell pepper strips and thyme sprigs to garnish
OLIVE PASTE:
1-1/4 cups pitted ripe olives (6 ounces)
2 tablespoons extra-virgin olive oil
Few drops of balsamic vinegar
Freshly ground pepper

Preheat oven to 400F (205C). To make Olive Paste, put ingredients in a food processor or blender and process until fairly smooth. Transfer to a bowl and set aside.

Cut each slice of bread into 3 strips. Place on a baking sheet and bake in preheated oven 10 to 12 minutes until golden and crisp. Meanwhile, warm oil with garlic in a small saucepan.

Drizzle oil and garlic over toasted bread. Spread with Olive Paste and serve at once garnished with bell pepper strips and thyme sprigs.

Makes 4 to 6 servings.

Note: Olive Paste can be made in advance or in larger quantities. Put into jars, add olive oil to cover and seal. Cover jars and keep in refrigerator up to 1 month.

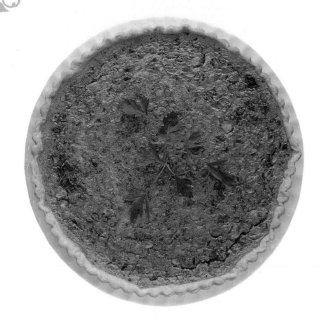

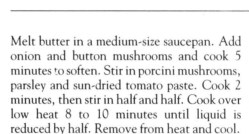

MUSHROOM TART

2 cups all-purpose flour
Pinch salt
1/2 cup butter, chilled, diced
About 5 tablespoons water
FILLING:
1 ounce dried porcini mushrooms
2 tablespoons butter
1 medium-size onion, finely chopped
4 ounces button mushrooms, chopped
2 tablespoons finely chopped Italian parsley
1 tablespoon sun-dried tomato paste
1/4 cup half and half
3 large eggs
1/4 cup freshly grated Parmesan cheese (3/4 ounce)
Salt and freshly ground pepper
Italian parsley sprig to garnish

Melt butter in a medium-size saucepan. Add onion and button mushrooms and cook 5 minutes to soften. Stir in porcini mushrooms, parsley and sun-dried tomato paste. Cook 2 minutes, then stir in half and half. Cook over low heat 8 to 10 minutes until liquid is reduced by half. Remove from heat and cool.

Sift flour and salt into a medium-size bowl. Rub butter in until mixture resembles bread crumbs. Stir in enough water to make a firm dough. Wrap in plastic wrap and refrigerate while preparing filling.

Roll out the dough and use to line greased pie pan. Prick bottom with a fork. Line pie shell with waxed paper and fill with dry beans. Bake in preheated oven 25 minutes, removing beans and paper last 5 minutes. Reduce temperature to 375F (190C).

Preheat oven to 400F (205C). Grease a 9-inch pie pan. Put porcini in a small bowl. Cover generously with warm water. Let soak 20 minutes, then drain and rinse to remove any grit. Dry on paper towels, then chop finely and set aside.

Beat eggs in a large bowl. Stir in mushroom mixture and cheese. Season with salt and freshly ground pepper, then pour into pie shell. Bake about 20 minutes until set. Serve warm or cold garnished with parsley sprig.

Makes 8 servings.

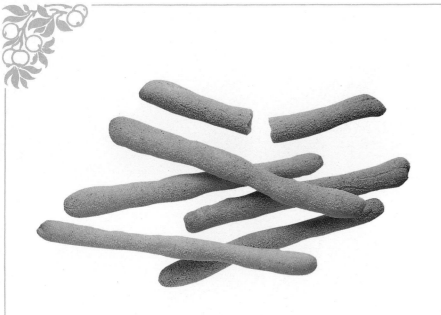

BREADSTICKS

4 cups bread flour or all-purpose flour
1/2 teaspoon salt
1/4 cup grated Parmesan cheese or provolone cheese
1 (1/4-oz.) package active dry yeast (about
   1 tablespoon)
1 teaspoon sugar
1-1/4 cups warm water (110F, 45C)
2 tablespoons extra-virgin olive oil plus extra for oiling
3/4 cup polenta or coarse cornmeal

Lightly oil a baking sheet. Roll out dough to a large rectangle and transfer to the baking sheet. Brush surface with a little oil, cover loosely with plastic wrap and let rise in a warm place 35 to 40 minutes until doubled in size. Preheat oven to 450F (230C). Lightly oil 2 more baking sheets. Cut dough into 24 equal pieces. Sprinkle polenta or cornmeal onto work surface. Using your hands, roll each piece of dough into a long thin rope about 9 inches long, coating thoroughly in polenta or cornmeal.

Sift flour and salt into a large bowl. Stir in cheese. In a small bowl, dissolve yeast and sugar in warm water. Let stand 5 to 10 minutes until frothy.

Arrange slightly apart on the baking sheets and bake in preheated oven 15 to 20 minutes until golden and crisp. Cool on wire racks. Serve warm or cold as part of the antipasti.

Makes 24 breadsticks.

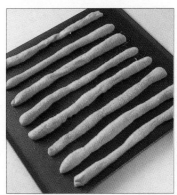

Stir the 2 tablespoons olive oil into yeast mixture. Using a wooden spoon, gradually beat yeast mixture into flour to give a soft dough. Knead dough on a floured surface 5 minutes until smooth and elastic.

Variation: Replace polenta or cornmeal with 3 ounces sesame seeds.

DEVILED CRAB QUICHE

2 cups all-purpose flour
1/2 teaspoon salt
1/2 teaspoon chili seasoning
1/4 cup cold margarine, diced
1/4 cup lard, diced
1/2 cup (2 oz.) finely grated Cheddar cheese
3 tablespoons cold water
6 slices bacon, chopped
1 onion, chopped
4 ounces crabmeat, flaked
3 eggs
2/3 cup half and half
1/2 teaspoon mustard powder
1/4 teaspoon cayenne pepper
Salt to taste
Tomato slices, if desired
Fresh Italian parsley sprigs, if desired

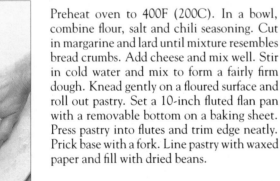

Preheat oven to 400F (200C). In a bowl, combine flour, salt and chili seasoning. Cut in margarine and lard until mixture resembles bread crumbs. Add cheese and mix well. Stir in cold water and mix to form a fairly firm dough. Knead gently on a floured surface and roll out pastry. Set a 10-inch fluted flan pan with a removable bottom on a baking sheet. Press pastry into flutes and trim edge neatly. Prick base with a fork. Line pastry with waxed paper and fill with dried beans.

Bake 15 minutes. Remove waxed paper and beans and bake 5 to 10 minutes more or until dry and lightly golden. Fry bacon 3 minutes. Add onion; cook 2 minutes. Remove from heat; mix with crabmeat. Spoon mixture into flan shell. Whisk eggs, half and half, mustard, cayenne and salt. Pour into flan shell. Bake 30 to 35 minutes or until set and lightly golden. Garnish with tomato and parsley, if desired, and serve warm or cold.

Makes 6 to 8 servings.

CHILI PEPPER PIZZA

3 tablespoons olive oil
1 onion, cut in fourths, sliced
1 clove garlic, crushed
1 (8 oz.) can tomatoes
1 tablespoon tomato paste
1/2 teaspoon dried oregano
1 cup all-purpose flour
1 cup whole-wheat flour
1/4 teaspoon salt
1 teaspoon active dried yeast
2/3 cup warm water (120F-130F/50C-55C)
1 (3-1/2-oz.) can green chilies
6 ounces Mozzarella cheese, chopped
2 ounces pepperoni or salami stick, sliced
8 ripe or green olives
Tomato roses, if desired
Fresh parsley sprigs, if desired

Lightly grease a 10-inch pizza pan. Heat 2 tablespoons of oil in a saucepan. Add onion, garlic, tomato paste, tomatoes with juice and oregano. Stir well to break up tomatoes, then simmer, uncovered, 10 to 15 minutes or until well thickened; cool. Preheat oven to 375F (190C). Put flours, salt and yeast in a bowl and mix well. Add water and mix to form a dough. Knead well, then roll to a 10-inch circle. Line greased pizza pan with dough.

Brush surface of dough with a little of remaining oil and cover with tomato mixture. Drain and chop chilies and sprinkle on top. Sprinkle with cheese and drizzle with remaining oil. Bake in preheated oven 25 minutes. Top pizza with pepperoni or salami and olives and bake 10 minutes. Cut in wedges. Garnish with tomato roses and parsley sprigs, if desired, and serve hot.

Makes 2 to 4 servings.

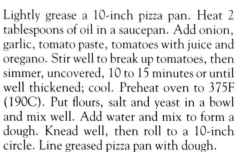

LAMB TRIANGLES

1 tablespoon vegetable oil
1 garlic clove, crushed
1 teaspoon grated fresh gingerroot
1 onion, finely chopped
1 tablespoon curry powder
1 tablespoon white-wine vinegar
1/2 lb. ground cooked lamb
1/2 cup water
2 tablespoons chopped fresh mint
Salt to taste
1 egg, beaten
3 sheets filo pastry
1/2 cup butter, melted

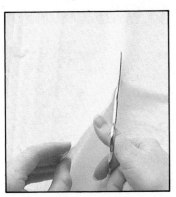

Heat oil in a large skillet over low heat. Add garlic, gingerroot and onion; cook for 1 minute, stirring. Add curry powder and cook for 1 more minute, stirring. Stir in vinegar, ground lamb and water, then simmer for 5 minutes. Add mint and salt. Remove from heat. Mix in egg; cool. Preheat oven to 400F (200C); lightly grease baking sheets. Cut pastry in 2-inch strips.

Work with 1 double strip of pastry at a time, keeping remaining pastry covered with a damp paper towel or plastic wrap to prevent drying. Brush 1 strip with melted butter. Place a spoonful of lamb in one corner and fold to form a triangle.

Continue folding, keeping the shape, until whole strip is used; press to seal and brush top with melted butter. Repeat with remaining pastry. Place on baking sheets; bake 20 minutes. Serve warm.

Makes 30 to 35.

MUSHROOM PASTIES

1 cup plus 1 tablespoon all-purpose flour
6 tablespoons firm butter
1 to 2 tablespoons cold water
3 green onions, chopped
1/2 lb. small fresh mushrooms, chopped
1/4 teaspoon dry mustard
1 tablespoon dry sherry
2 tablespoons milk
8 pitted ripe olives, sliced
Salt and pepper to taste
1 egg, beaten

Sift 1 cup flour into a bowl. Using a pastry blender or 2 knives, cut in 4 tablespoons butter until mixture resembles coarse crumbs. Sprinkle in cold water, stirring with a fork until dough holds together. Gather into a ball; wrap and chill 30 minutes.

Melt remaining 2 tablespoons butter in a large skillet. Add green onions and cook, stirring, until soft but not browned. Add mushrooms and cook, stirring, until all liquid has evaporated. Stir in remaining 1 tablespoon flour; then stir in mustard, sherry and milk. Bring to a boil, stirring. Stir in olives and season. Remove from heat. Chill.

Preheat oven to 400F (200C). Grease 2 baking sheets. On a floured board, roll out pastry thinly and cut into 3-inch rounds. Place a teaspoonful of filling in center of each round. Brush up edges and join in center; pinch. Brush tops with egg. Bake 15 to 20 minutes.

Makes 10.

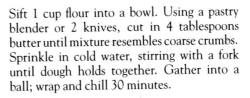

RICOTTA-CHEESE BALLS

2 lbs. ricotta cheese (4 cups), well chilled
1 red bell pepper, seeded, finely chopped
1/4 cup finely chopped mixed fresh herbs (including
    some green onion, if desired)
1/4 cup black sesame seeds or finely chopped pistachio
    nuts
1 teaspoon salt

Line a baking sheet or tray with plastic wrap. Using a small ice-cream scoop, shape ricotta cheese into 24 equal balls. Divide ricotta balls into 3 groups of 8 balls each. Roll 1 group in chopped bell pepper.

Roll second group of balls in chopped herbs.

Mix sesame seeds or pistachios and salt, spread on a sheet of wax paper. Roll remaining 8 balls in nut or seed mixture. Arrange all balls on lined baking sheets; cover and refrigerate until ready to serve. To serve, arrange ricotta balls in rows on a platter.

Makes 24.

Tip: Black sesame seeds are available in Asian grocery stores.

SPINACH & FETA ROLLS

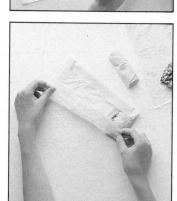

2 tablespoons vegetable oil
2 onions, finely chopped
1 (10-oz.) pkg. frozen chopped spinach, thawed
2 teaspoons dried dill weed
4 oz. feta cheese, crumbled
1 egg, beaten
3 tablespoons dairy sour cream
12 sheets filo pastry
1/2 cup butter, melted

Heat oil in a saucepan over low heat. Add onions and cook, stirring occasionally, until soft but not browned. Meanwhile, drain spinach well, then place in a colander and press out as much water as possible. Stir spinach into onions and cook 2 minutes longer. Stir in dill weed and cheese.

Remove from heat; cool. Mix in egg and sour cream. Cover and refrigerate until cold. Preheat oven to 400F (200C). Work with 2 sheets of pastry at a time, keeping remaining pastry covered with damp paper towels or plastic wrap to prevent drying. Brush 1 sheet with melted butter. Top with another sheet; cut stacked sheets crosswise in 3 strips.

Place a spoonful of filling at 1 end of each strip; tuck in sides and roll up. Brush ends of rolls with melted butter; press lightly to seal. Repeat with remaining sheets of pastry to make 15 more rolls. Place rolls, seam-side down, on baking sheets. Bake about 15 minutes or until golden brown. Serve hot.

Makes 18.

CURRY PIES

HOT CHEESE & HAM PUFFS

1 tablespoon vegetable oil
1 onion, chopped
1 lb. lean ground beef
1 tablespoon curry powder
2 tablespoons distilled white vinegar
6 tablespoons water
1 teaspoon salt
2 tablespoons seedless golden raisins
2 teaspoons cornstarch
1/2 lb. short pastry
1 egg, beaten

Heat oil in large skillet. Add onion, then crumble in beef. Cook, stirring 2 minutes. Add curry powder; cook, stirring, 1 more minute. Stir in vinegar, 4 tablespoons water, salt and raisins. Reduce heat, cover and simmer 10 minutes.

Stir together cornstarch and remaining 2 tablespoons water; stir into meat mixture. Cook, stirring, about 2 minutes. Remove from heat; cool, then refrigerate until cold.

Preheat oven to 400F (200C). Lightly grease 12 to 15 tart pans. On a lightly floured board, roll out 1/2 of pastry thinly. Cut into 12 to 15 rounds and fit into greased 2-inch tart pans. Spoon cold meat mixture into pastry shells. Roll out remaining pastry, cut into rounds and place on tarts; trim edges and press with a fork to seal. Brush tops of tarts with egg or water, then prick each several times. Bake about 15 minutes.

Makes 12 to 15.

1/2 cup plus 1 tablespoon all-purpose flour
1/2 cup water
1/2 teaspoon salt
1/4 cup butter, cut in pieces
2 eggs
2 tablespoons butter
1/2 cup milk
3 tablespoons shredded Cheddar cheese
About 1/2 cup chopped cooked ham
3 tablespoons freshly grated Parmesan cheese

Preheat oven to 400F (200C). Grease 2 baking sheets. Sift 1/2 cup flour onto a sheet of waxed paper. Heat water, the salt and 1/4 cup butter until butter melts.

Bring to a full boil; add sifted flour all at once. Stir over low heat about 1 minute or until mixture leaves sides of pan and forms a ball. Remove from heat; cool slightly. Beat in eggs, 1 at a time, beating until smooth after each addition. Drop batter by heaping tea-spoonfuls onto baking sheets. Bake 25 to 30 minutes or until puffy. Cool on racks. Cut each puff in half; scoop out soft centers. Melt 2 tablespoons butter over low heat. Stir in 1 tablespoon flour and milk. Continue to cook, stirring, until sauce thickens. Add Cheddar cheese and stir until melted, then stir in ham. Remove from heat; season.

Spoon into bottom halves of puffs, then replace tops. Arrange on baking sheets. Sprinkle with Parmesan cheese. Bake 5 minutes.

Makes 20.

—SMOKED-SALMON QUICHES—

1/2 (17-1/4-oz.) pkg. frozen puff pastry, thawed
6 eggs
1-1/2 cups whipping cream
1/2 teaspoon salt
Pinch of ground nutmeg
1/4 lb. smoked salmon, chopped
Black caviar, smoked salmon and dill sprigs, if desired

Preheat oven to 400F (200C). Grease twenty-four 2-inch tart pans. Unfold pastry sheets; place one on a lightly floured board, roll out slightly and cut into 24 rounds. Fit pastry rounds into greased tart pans.

In a bowl, beat eggs, cream, salt and nutmeg until blended. Stir in 1/4 pound chopped salmon. Spoon mixture into the pastry-lined pans, making sure salmon is evenly distributed.

Bake 10 to 15 minutes or until filling is puffed and golden. Carefully remove from pans; if desired, garnish with caviar, titbits of salmon and dill sprigs. Serve warm. If prepared ahead, remove quiches from pans, cool completely on racks, cover and refrigerate. To reheat, arrange on baking sheets; bake in a 400F (200C) oven about 5 minutes or until heated through. Garnish.

Makes 24.

—ARTICHOKES WITH CAVIAR—

1 (14 oz.) can artichoke bottoms packed in water
3 to 6 slices firm-textured bread
2 tablespoons vegetable oil
2 tablespoons dairy sour cream
1 tablespoon mayonnaise, preferably homemade
Lemon juice to taste
1 tablespoon chopped chives
2 tablespoons black or red caviar
Dill sprigs if desired

Drain artichoke bottoms in a sieve; pat dry with paper towels. Cut bread slices into 2-1/2-inch rounds; you will need 6 bread rounds. Reserve bread trimmings for bread crumbs or other uses, if desired.

Heat oil in a skillet, add bread rounds and cook, turning as needed, until golden on both sides. Drain on paper towels. If prepared ahead, cool; then store in an airtight container up to 24 hours.

In a bowl, stir together sour cream, mayonnaise, lemon juice and chives. cover and refrigerate until ready to serve. To assemble, arrange 1 artichoke bottom on each toasted bread round. Top each with a spoonful of the sour-cream mixture and 1 teaspoon caviar. If desired, garnish with dill sprigs.

Makes 6.

QUICK DIPS

CREAM CORN DIP

1 (10-oz.) jar corn relish
1-1/4 cups dairy sour cream
Crackers or corn chips

Stir together corn relish and sour cream, then spoon into a serving bowl. Serve with crackers or corn chips for dipping.

Makes about 1-1/2 cups.

CAVIAR DIP

1-1/4 cups dairy sour cream
1 tablespoon finely chopped onion
1 (2-oz.) jar red caviar
Italian parsley
Crackers or crisp raw vegetables

Stir together sour cream, onion and 1/2 of caviar, then spoon into a serving bowl. Swirl in remaining caviar. Garnish and serve with crackers or vegetables for dipping.

Makes about 1-1/4 cups.

ANCHOVY DIP

1 (2-oz.) can flat anchovy fillets, drained
1-1/4 cups dairy sour cream
3 tablespoons chopped dill pickle
2 teaspoons drained capers
Crackers

Coarsely chop anchovies, then mash well. Stir together sour cream, anchovies and pickle, then spoon into a serving bowl. Garnish with capers. Serve with crackers for dipping.

Makes about 1-1/2 cups.

ORIENTAL GINGERED SHRIMP

8 unshelled raw jumbo shrimp, thawed if frozen
1/2 cup all-purpose flour
1/4 teaspoon salt
1 teaspoon corn oil
1/4 cup water
1 (1-inch) piece gingerroot, peeled, grated
1 clove garlic, crushed
1 teaspoon chili, sauce
1 egg white
Vegetable oil
1 green onion daisy
Red bell pepper strips

Shell shrimp, leaving tail shells on. Make a small incision along spines. Remove black spinal cord from shrimp.

In a bowl, combine flour, salt, corn oil and water. Stir in ginger, garlic and chili sauce and beat well. Stiffly whisk egg white, then gently fold into batter until evenly combined.

Half fill a deep-fat fryer or saucepan with oil; heat to 375F (190C) or until a 1/2-inch cube of day-old bread browns in 40 seconds. Hold each shrimp by its tail and dip into batter, then lower into hot oil. Fry 3 minutes or until golden. Drain on paper towels. Garnish with green onion daisy and bell pepper strips and serve hot.

Makes 4 servings.

PEANUT SAUCE

2 garlic cloves
2 tablespoons dark soy sauce
1/4 cup smooth peanut butter
1 tablespoon sugar
1 cup water
2 small, fresh, red hot chilies, seeded
Crisp raw vegetables, such as carrots, celery,
   cucumbers, green beans, small whole radishes,
   cauliflowerets (blanched, if desired) and edible-
   pod peas

Crush garlic into a small saucepan with the soy sauce, peanut butter, sugar and water.

Cut the chilies in small slivers and add to the saucepan. Bring to a simmer; then simmer 5 minutes, stirring constantly. If sauce is very thin, simmer until slightly thickened. Remove from heat; cool to room temperature before serving. If sauce solidifies upon cooling, thin it with a little hot water.

Prepare vegetables; cut carrots, celery and cucumber into 2-inch pieces, then cut in thin strips. To serve, pour sauce into a serving bowl and place in center of a platter. Arrange vegetables of your choice around sauce. Dip vegetables in sauce before eating.

Makes about 1/4 cup sauce.

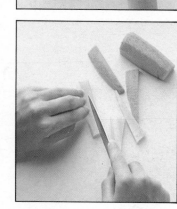

MEXICAN BEAN DIP

1 (15-oz.) can red kidney beans
2 tablespoons vegetable oil
3/4 cup shredded Cheddar cheese (3 oz.)
Salt to taste
1 teaspoon chili powder
1 tablespoon chopped green bell pepper
Deep-fried shrimp chips, see below

Drain beans, reserving liquid.

Heat oil in a medium skillet; add drained beans and heat through, mashing with a potato masher or fork. Add 3 tablespoons reserved bean liquid and stir well. Remove from heat; cool. Stir in cheese, salt and chili powder. Heat through over low heat. If mixture is too thick, stir in more reserved bean liquid until mixture has a good consistency for scooping with chips. Stir in bell pepper. Serve dip hot, with corn or deep-fried shrimp chips.

Makes about 1-1/2 cups.

DEEP FRIED SHRIMP CHIPS
Shrimp chips are available from Asian grocery stores. Drop a few at a time into deep hot oil and when they come to the surface, remove at once; chips take only a few seconds to cook. Drain on paper towels; store in an airtight container until ready to serve.

HUMMUS BI TAHINI

1/2 cup plus 1 tablespoon dried garbanzo beans
About 2 teaspoons salt
4 garlic cloves
1/2 cup tahini
Lemon juice to taste
About 1 tablespoon olive oil
Paprika and Italian parsley sprigs
Pocket bread, cut in wedges

Rinse and sort beans, then soak overnight in cold water to cover.

Drain and place in a saucepan. Pour in enough cold water to cover; stir in 2 teaspoons salt. Bring to a boil; reduce heat, cover and simmer 2 hours or until beans are very tender. Drain, reserving cooking liquid. Place drained beans in a food processor fitted with a metal blade. Process to make a smooth paste, adding a little reserved cooking liquid as needed. Add garlic, tahini and lemon juice. Process until blended. Add salt.

Turn hummus into a serving bowl, smooth surface and drizzle with enough oil to make a thin layer (this prevents drying). Garnish with paprika and 1 or 2 Italian parsley sprigs. Serve with pocket-bread wedges.

Serves 12 to 15.

Variation: If desired, split pocket bread, tear in pieces and bake in a 300F (150C) oven 10 to 15 minutes or until crisp.

EGG & NORI ROLLS

3 sheets nori (dried laver seaweed)
3 eggs
Pinch of salt
1 tablespoon cold water

Toast each sheet of nori until crisp by running it quickly back and forth over a gas flame or above an electric element set on medium heat. Be careful not to burn nori. Set toasted nori aside.

In a bowl, beat together eggs, salt and water. Heat a skillet on a medium heat; grease lightly. Set 1 teaspoon egg mixture aside. Use the remaining egg mixture to make 4 thin omelets. Trim nori sheets to same size as omelets.

Place omelet, uncooked-side up, on a bamboo mat. Top with 1 sheet nori. Continue stacking omelets and nori sheets until all are used. Roll up omelet-nori stack in mat to make a tight, compact cylinder; seal seam with reserved egg mixture. Let stand until cold. Remove bamboo mat; cut roll in chunks.

Makes about 12.

Tip: Nori is dried laver seaweed. The greenish-black sheets are sold in Asian grocery stores and some well-stocked supermarkets.

SKEWERED BITES

PROSCIUTTO & MELON

1 small cantaloupe
1/2 lb. very thinly sliced prosciutto

Peel melon, cut in half and scoop out seeds. Cut flesh in cubes. To make each skewer, gather up a slice of prosciutto and skewer onto a melon cube with a wooden pick. Refrigerate until chilled, then serve.

Makes about 48.

AVOCADO & SHRIMP

1 ripe avocado
1 lb. cooked large or jumbo shrimp, shelled, deveined
Lemon juice

Halve and pit avocado. Scoop flesh from each half with a melon-ball cutter; or peel halves, then cut in cubes. Skewer 1 shrimp and 1 avocado piece on each wooden pick. Sprinkle with lemon juice and serve immediately.

Makes about 18.

SMOKED-BEEF ROLLS

2 tablespoons dairy sour cream
1 teaspoon prepared horseradish
1/4 lb. thinly sliced smoked beef

Stir together sour cream and horseradish. Spread mixture on beef slices; roll up, slice and cut in 1-inch pieces. Skewer 2 or 3 pieces on each wooden pick.

Makes 8 to 10.

MINTED SAMBAL DIP

4 green onions
1-1/4 cups dairy sour cream
1 teaspoon finely grated fresh gingerroot
1 tablespoon lemon juice
1 tablespoon curry powder
1/2 cup chopped fresh mint
1 garlic clove
1 teaspoon salt
Celery and other crisp vegetables

With a sharp knife, finely chop green onion, including tops. In a large bowl, mix together chopped green onion, sour cream, grated gingerroot, lemon juice, curry powder and chopped mint.

Use the tip of a strong knife to crush the garlic in salt until it forms a pulp; add to dairy sour cream mixture. If mixture is thin, whip until thickened and stir well. Cover and refrigerate at least 24 hours.

To serve, prepare vegetables for crudités; cut celery sticks in 4-inch thin strips. Place the dip in the center of a platter and surround with the vegetables for dipping.

Serves 4.

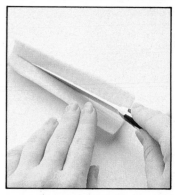

DEVILED MIXED NUTS

3/4 cup whole almonds
1 cup raw cashews
1 cup pecan halves
3 tablespoons butter
2 garlic cloves, crushed
1 teaspoon Worcestershire sauce
2 teaspoons curry powder
Pinch of red (cayenne) pepper

To blanch almonds, pour boiling water over nuts in a heatproof bowl, leave a few minutes, then lift out. The nuts will easily slip out of the skins.

Preheat oven to 350F (180C). Place almonds, cashew and pecans in a bowl. Melt butter in a saucepan and stir in garlic, Worcestershire sauce, curry powder and red pepper. Drizzle butter mixture evenly over nuts and toss to coat evenly.

Spread nuts in a baking dish; bake 15 to 20 minutes, or until golden, stirring every 5 minutes to toast evenly. Remove from oven and cool. Store in an airtight container until ready to serve.

Makes about 3 cups.

SPICED CRACKED OLIVES

2 lbs. large green olives, drained
2-3 small, whole, dried red hot chilies
4 garlic cloves
3 dill sprigs
3 thyme sprigs
3 oregano sprigs
2 teaspoons fennel seeds
Olive oil

Make a lengthwise cut in each olive, cutting in as far as the pit. (This allows flavors from the marinade to penetrate.)

Place olives, chilies, garlic, dill sprigs, thyme sprigs, oregano sprigs and fennel seeds in a large jar. Pour in enough oil to cover. Cover jar tightly; refrigerate at least several days before serving. Drain; serve as an appetizer with drinks or use in salads. You may reserve oil and add more olives to it; or use oil for cooking or in salad dressings.

Makes about 1-3/4 lb.

CALAMATTA OLIVES WITH GARLIC
Calamatta olives
Garlic cloves
Small, whole, dried red hot chilies, if desired
Olive oil (or half olive oil, half vegetable oil)

In a jar, combine olives and garlic cloves. Add a few chilies for added bite, if desired. Pour in enough oil to cover olives. Cover jar tightly and refrigerate at least several days before serving. Drain; serve with drinks.

ASPARAGUS ROLLS

25 fresh or canned asparagus spears
1 cup butter
4 egg yolks
1 tablespoon chopped fresh mint
Lemon juice to taste
25 thin slices firm-textured white bread

If using fresh asparagus, snap off and discard tough stalk ends. Wash stalks in cold water, then cook about 8 minutes in boiling water. Drain, rinse under cold running water and drain again. If using canned asparagus, drain well. Set asparagus aside.

To make sauce, melt butter in a small saucepan and keep very hot. Process egg yolks in a food processor fitted with a metal blade until frothy. With motor running, gradually add hot melted butter in a thin stream; process until blended. Transfer to a bowl; cover and refrigerate until mixture is thickened. Stir in mint and lemon juice.

Preheat broiler. Trim crusts from bread slices, then spread bread with sauce. Cut each asparagus spear in half; place 2 halves on each bread slice. Bring 2 opposite corners to center of each slice; fasten with a wooden pick. Dot with more sauce. Arrange asparagus rolls on a baking sheet; broil until crisp and golden.

Makes 25.

CUCUMBER SANDWICHES

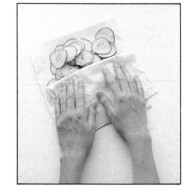

2 cucumbers
1 tablespoon salt
24 thin slices firm-textured white or wholewheat bread
1/2 cup butter, room temperature
Freshly ground pepper to taste
3 tablespoons dairy sour cream
1 bunch chives, chopped

Thinly slice cucumbers. (If using a tough-skinned variety, peel and seed before slicing.) Arrange cucumber slices in a single layer of a flat platter or in a large rimmed baking dish. Sprinkle with salt. Cover cucumber slices with a plate (or plates); top plate with a weight, such as canned goods. Let stand several hours.

Drain all juices from cucumber slices; then rinse under cold running water to remove excess salt. Drain well between several layers of paper towels. Cover and refrigerate until ready to use.

Trim crusts from bread slices; spread 1 side of each slice with butter. Top buttered side of 12 slices with cucumber slices; sprinkle with pepper. Cover with remaining bread slices, buttered-side down. Cut each sandwich diagonally in quarters. Spread sour cream on 1 cut side of each triangle, then dip in chives. Arrange on a platter and serve.

Makes 48.

DOLMADES

1 (8-oz.) jar grape leaves
2 tablespoons olive oil
1 onion, finely chopped
2 cups cooked long-grain white rice
Salt and pepper to taste
2 tablespoons chopped fresh mint
1 cup toasted pine nuts
Fresh mint sprigs if desired

Drain grape leaves and rinse well; then soak in cold water to cover to remove brine, separating leaves carefully. Drain and set aside.

Heat oil in a medium skillet. Add onion and cook, stirring, until tender. Remove from heat and stir in rice, salt, pepper, mint and 1/2 cup toasted pine nuts. Place about 2 teaspoons filling on each leaf; roll up leaf, tucking in edges.

Arrange filled leaves close together in large skillet. If necessary, make more than 1 layer; separate layers with left-over grape leaves. pour in enough hot water to barely cover filled leaves. Place a heatproof plate directly on top of leaves; place a weight (such as canned goods) on top of plate. Cover and simmer 30 minutes. Remove from heat; cool. Cover and refrigerate until cold. Garnish with 1/2 cup toasted pine nuts or fresh mint sprigs, if desired.

Makes about 45.

GINGERED FRUIT KEBABS

1 cantaloupe or honeydew melon (or some of each)
About 1 pint fresh strawberries
1-3/4 cups dairy sour cream or plain yogurt
1 tablespoon honey
1 tablespoon chopped crystallized ginger
1 tablespoon chopped fresh mint
Mint sprigs, if desired

Peel melon; cut in half, scoop out seeds and cut flesh in bite-size pieces. Wash and hull strawberries; halve.

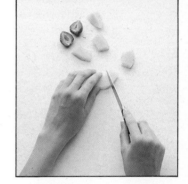

Thread fruit on about 20 bamboo skewers, alternating melon chunks and berries. If preparing ahead, arrange skewered fruits in a container, cover and refrigerate up to 4 hours.

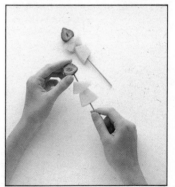

In a small bowl, stir together, sour cream or yogurt, honey, ginger and chopped mint. Cover and refrigerate until ready to serve, then transfer to a serving bowl. Place bowl in center of a platter; surround with fruit kebabs. If desired, garnish with mint sprigs. Dip fruit in sour-cream sauce before eating.

Makes about 20.

Tip: In place of melon and strawberries, you may use any suitable fruit in season – pineapple, apples, pears or citrus fruit, for example.

Index